HOMES WITH HARMONY

I0149565

DR. LINDSEY GARMON

21ST CENTURY CHRISTIAN

ISBN: 978-0-89098-368-3
Copyright © 2008 by 21st Century Christian
2809 Granny White Pike, Nashville, TN.

Cover Design By Martell Speigner

Dedicated To My Wonderful Wife

Sherrie Angell Garmon

With Whom I Have Enjoyed
Many Years Of Marital Harmony

A wife of noble character who can find?
She is worth far more than rubies.
Her husband has full confidence in her
and lacks nothing of value.
She brings him good, not harm,
all the days of her life.

Proverbs 31:10-12

Recommendations For *Homes With Harmony*

Dr. Garmon has written a very practical guide for strengthening marriages. His material is Biblically based, accurate, and easy to read. What is particularly helpful are the "Harmony Building Exercises" at the end of each chapter. Couples who take this material seriously cannot help but talk about important issues and changes that may need to occur to make their marriages more harmonious.

— Dr. Frank Scott, Family Life Minister
Madison, Tennessee

As a Christian couple, we have studied the material in *Homes with Harmony* and found it to be a joyous and soulful book. These lessons have reminded us of how important the basics of a loving and Spirit-filled relationship are. Lindsey has a gift for making complex situations seem simple again. Prior to our exposure to these lessons, we did not realize how many "rooms" in our "communication house" (see chapter 3) we were not able to freely enter. Now, we are learning to open a new door together every day.

— Sam & Vanessa Dorbandt
Portland, Texas

Homes with Harmony is a very balanced and valuable book on living and loving our families. One impressive trait about this book is that it is easy to read even though Dr. Garmon reveals information that is often complex. I'm going to recommend [it] again and again to new and established families in my life because I believe it provides a uniquely important guide for today's husbands, wives, and parents.

— Lee Wilson, Family Dynamics Institute
Editor of GraceCentered.com

Someone has defined the word "kissing" as "a means of getting two people so close together that they can't see anything wrong with each other." Of course once you are married, those faults become all too apparent. A good marriage requires that we deal with our flaws and work hard to build a relationship that is real and lasting. Lindsey gives us real tools, Biblical and practical, to work through the issues that must be dealt with in order to create harmonious homes.

— Ross Thomson, Pulpit Minister
Houston, Texas

TABLE OF CONTENTS

Introduction..7

Chapter 1
The Marriage Merger—Harmony Or Havoc?..........................11

Chapter 2
Sorting Out The "We" And "Me"—Can There Be Harmony?.....19

Chapter 3
The Quest For Harmony In Marital Communication (Part 1)....27

Chapter 4
The Quest For Harmony In Marital Communication (Part 2)....37

Chapter 5
The Quest For Harmony In Marital Communication (Part 3)....47

Chapter 6
Harmony In Marital Finances..57

Chapter 7
Harmony In Marital Romance..71

Chapter 8
Sexual Harmony In Marriage...79

Chapter 9
Harmony With The In-Laws...91

Chapter 10
When Harmony Is Threatened—Dealing With Conflict And Anger....103

Chapter 11
Child-Rearing—Preserving Harmony In The Midst Of Hassles.....117

Chapter 12
The Most Beautiful Harmony Of All—Spiritual Intimacy.......129

INTRODUCTION

Understanding The Word..."Harmony"

If you compare the wording in various dictionaries, you will find the word "harmony" defined in a way similar to this:

> **Harmony** (har'mo-ne) n. – 1. A combination of *different parts* into a pleasing or orderly whole. 2. A careful arranging of *diverse elements* to form a pleasant unit. 3. Applied to music, harmony is the simultaneous sounding of two or more *distinct tones* that, combined, create a sound that is satisfying to the ear.

You create "harmony" when you take—*different parts...diverse elements...distinct components...*and blend them together so as to create something that is—*pleasing...orderly...pleasant...and satisfying.* Using these same descriptive words, we can say that homes with harmony are family settings in which very different individuals learn to co-exist in ways that are generally *pleasing, orderly, pleasant, and satisfying.*

Living together in "harmony" is not the same as living together in "unison." The word "unison" means, "actions that are completely uniform." When humans act in "unison," they think, speak, and act identically. When two people sing in "unison," they sing the same notes at the same time.

"Harmony" is different. When two people sing in "harmony," they make very different tones that are blended to create a sound that is pleasing and pleasant to the ears. We can never live in homes with unison. We can, however, learn to live in homes with harmony!

Harmony In The Home—A Great Challenge

When God designed the family, He began by uniting two very different specimens—a man and a woman. How different are we? Our differences can, at times, feel like we are from different planets—Mars and Venus. The reality, however, is that both men and women are from planet Earth—the miraculous and marvelous creations of God. Still, we are very different in every cell of our bodies—the anatomy is different, the hormones are different, and the emotions are different. Learning to live harmoniously with these differences is one of life's greatest challenges.

Let's Look Forward—Not Backward

This study will promote the biblical principle that harmony in the home is greatly enhanced when husbands and wives are committed to the truth that marriage is to be a permanent relationship. God's plan and desire is for marriage to last a lifetime.

While stressing the permanency of marriage, we are sensitive to and aware of the reality that, for some, relational harmony has already been broken. Melody may have turned to misery along the way. The intent in this material is not to re-open old wounds or revive feelings of pain and failure from the past. We simply cannot journey back in history and relive those painful days or remake those important decisions. What we can and must do, however, is rely upon God's grace and experience new beginnings. Starting today, we can go forward practicing marital commitment and building strong homes of health and harmony for the future.

Harmony Requires "A Concert"—Not "A Contest"

In a contest, the opposing parts compete with each other. In a concert, they complete each other. For example, in a musical concert, the tuba is not in competition with the trumpet. No! These two instruments, along with all the others, have one common goal—uniting their very different sounds under the leadership of one conductor so as to create one concordant sound, which results in beautiful harmony.

God wants your home to resemble "a concert"—not "a contest." The major goal must be "to complete"—not "compete." This can only happen when we submit ourselves to the authority and direction of our one great conductor—the Lord Jesus Christ. Following His plan for marriage and the family, we can experience "Homes With Harmony" and create beautiful relational music that will be an honor to heaven and a blessing to earth.

May God help us to have "Homes With Harmony!"

So God created man in his own image, in the image of God he created him; male and female he created them. . .God saw all that he had made, and it was very good. (Genesis 1:27, 31)

*The L*ORD *God said, "It is not good for the man to be alone. I will make a helper suitable for him." (Genesis 2:18)*

*So the man gave names to all the livestock, the birds of the air and all the beasts of the field. But for Adam no suitable helper was found. So the L*ORD *God caused the man to fall into a deep sleep; and while he was sleeping, he took one of the man's ribs and closed up the place with flesh. Then the L*ORD *God made a woman from the rib he had taken out of the man, and he brought her to the man. The man said,*

> *"This is now bone of my bones and flesh of my flesh; she shall be called 'woman,' for she was taken out of man." For this reason a man will leave his father and mother and be united to his wife, and they will become one flesh. (Genesis 2:20-24)*

CHAPTER 1
The Marriage Merger—Harmony Or Havoc?

Marriage—Life's Greatest Merger

We are living in a day of big mergers, but one of the biggest and most challenging mergers of all has to be the union of a man and a woman in marriage. The marriage merger is entered into with a simple "I do," and this may be the only simple thing about the entire process. Only the naïve could ever imagine that *"two becoming one"* would be an easy undertaking. As tough as a wedding can be, it is easier than the hard work required in marriage. The wedding occurs on one day. The marriage involves a lifetime.

Think about it! Two members of the opposite sex bring their backgrounds, beliefs, bodies, brains, bloodlines, belongings, bills, and burdens and merge them into what they hope will be the core of one big happy family! What a challenge! Someone has said, "The best place on earth to find optimists is in the waiting room of a Marriage License Office." The merging of two lives is never easy!

Can We Fathom The Enormity Of This Merger?

One young, inexperienced minister was preparing to officiate at his first wedding ceremony. He was nervous—extremely nervous. His greatest fear was that in the middle of the ceremony, he would go blank—forget what to say next. He decided to speak with an older, more experienced preacher about his nervousness. The older gentleman advised the young man to stay calm. He said, "If you go blank and forget what to say next during the ceremony, just begin to quote Scripture—whatever comes to your mind. Once you remember where you were in the ceremony, then you will be able to proceed." The young man was grateful for the advice and felt greatly relieved.

The day of the wedding came. As expected, he was very nervous and as feared, he went stone blank during the ceremony. Panic! What did he do? He did precisely what the older preacher had told him to do. He began to quote Scripture. And, the first words out of his mouth were, *"Father, forgive them. For they know not what they do."* The harsh reality is that no bride or groom fully comprehends the magnitude of the merger they are entering when they say, "I do!"

Help! Living With Another Human Is Not Easy!

Have you noticed? Human beings tend to be selfish, independent, and even domineering? Try sharing a bed, a bank account, a bathroom, and a TV remote and see what happens. These tendencies may reveal themselves in living color when we begin to interact in marriage. One wife said, "Things started to change the moment we cut the wedding cake." For many couples, there is a crash into major disappointment as they discover the "deep divide" that can exist in connection with temperaments, money, sex, chores, in-laws, time, friends, entertainment, space, and other areas where personal preferences frequently emerge. Differences that never surfaced during the courting phase can suddenly arise as high, thick walls that discourage and divide us. We soon discover that there are two ways of looking at things—your spouse's way and your way, also known as "the right way." One lady said, "I knew I married Mr. Right. I just did not know that his first name was 'Always' and his middle name was 'And Forever.'"

The Core Problem That Makes Merging Difficult

Many factors may explain the strains and struggles that arise when two people attempt to blend their lives. Every bride and groom bring baggage into their relationship—cultural, emotional, social, spiritual, and otherwise. Some of this baggage can be extremely heavy and burdensome. Why is it so difficult to unpack our baggage and live in harmony with each other?

At the very core of our struggles to *"become one"* is what the Bible refers to as the problem of the sinful nature. The painful fact is that in marriage, we each live with a sinner. Note what letter of the alphabet is at the center of the word "s 'I' n." The tendency to be self-centered and self-serving affects every human being and every marriage relationship. None of us had to go to school to learn how to be selfish. This tendency comes as standard equipment in the human species. He wants "his way." She demands "her way." The sinful nature is frequently at the core of our marriage struggles. Can you see how a self-serving spirit affects harmony in the home?

> *We all, like sheep, have gone astray, each of us has turned to his own way...(Isaiah 53:6)*

So I say, let the Holy Spirit guide your lives. Then you won't be doing what your sinful nature craves. The sinful nature wants to do evil, which is just the opposite of what the Spirit wants. And the Spirit gives us desires that are the opposite of what the sinful nature desires. These two forces are constantly fighting each other, so you are not free to carry out your good intentions. (Galatians 5:16-17 NLT)

As for you, you were dead in your transgressions and sins, in which you used to live when you followed the ways of this world and of the ruler of the kingdom of the air, the spirit who is now at work in those who are disobedient. All of us also lived among them at one time, gratifying the cravings of our sinful nature and following its desires and thoughts. Like the rest, we were by nature objects of wrath. (Ephesians 2:1-3)

I know that nothing good lives in me, that is, in my sinful nature. For I have the desire to do what is good, but I cannot carry it out. For what I do is not the good I want to do; no, the evil I do not want to do—this I keep on doing. (Romans 7:18-19)

Even the strongest of Christian couples will inevitably find themselves engaged in a battle of wills as two powerful centers of self-assertion collide. It is a myth to believe that Christian marriages are free of conflict. However, through mutual submission to the Prince of Peace, Jesus, marriage can become a crucible in which these stubborn wills are melted and merged.

Other Factors That Mar Our Marriage Mergers

There are numerous other problems that complicate our efforts to merge two lives and create harmony in marriage. Let's mention four of these.

1. Our courting practices are flawed.

Someone has said, "Dating is marketing and courting is the process of closing the sale." When people date repeatedly, this evolves into courtship. "Courtship" should be what the word implies—treating someone "kingly" or "queenly" with the intent of convincing him or her to spend the rest of life with you.

The courtship process in our culture has weaknesses and flaws. Thus, what you see in courtship is not always what you get in marriage. True, the typical dating couple talks for hours and hours and they believe they know each other well. Yet, in many ways a dating relationship can actually conceal information rather than reveal it. Someone said, "Marriage is like deep sea fishing. You never know for sure what you have on the hook until you get it in the boat."

Some discover that they have married virtual strangers. Courtship is designed to eliminate the element of surprise, yet frequently we hear marriage partners say, "I had no idea he or she was like that!" The truth is that discovering and dealing with individual differences is a never-ending process for married people.

In some cases, courtship can be a period of time when each partner puts his or her best foot forward while hiding embarrassing facts, habits, flaws, and temperaments. We reveal our "social personalities" and conceal many of our "selfish beliefs and behaviors." Consequently, the bride and groom enter into marriage with an array of private assumptions about how life will be lived after the wedding. In time, major conflict breaks out when they discover that they differ radically on what each partner considers non-negotiable issues. This can be frightening to couples as they hit the wall of reality and realize that they have married an imperfect person. For some, this can lead to feelings of entrapment, anger, and despair. Harmony can turn into havoc!

2. Many of our role models are corrupted.

In recent decades, the divorce rate has been extremely high with approximately one-half of marriages splitting up. And sadly, for many of the couples that did manage to stay together, it was a story of "endurance"—not "enjoyment." Some toughed it out for the benefit of the children or social status. Incredibly, only a small percentage of couples have managed to achieve a high level of healthy intimacy in the marriage relationship.

In view of these realities, it is a fact that more couples are going into marriage having no healthy role models to instruct and inform them in their efforts to build solid relationships. The finest way for Christian husbands to learn how to treat their wives and for Christian wives to know how to relate to their husbands is to witness healthy married love being modeled within their homes of origin. Many have never seen such models and have grown up in environments where unhealthy and unholy patterns were the norm. Sadly, for many in our culture, the abnormal has become the normal. In a recent survey taken in a "small hometown setting," in the Bible belt, it was discovered that in the typical public middle school classroom, less than one-half of the students were still living in homes occupied by both biological parents.

Into this vacuum where role models are lacking, the television industry and Hollywood have flooded our culture with models that glorify and perpetuate behavior that is weak, perverted, and even violent. The lack of healthy role models in family life today has created huge gaps and deep holes that make it difficult to navigate on the road that leads to marital harmony.

3. Our depth of commitment is shallow.

Commitment in marriage is a deep resolve to stand, stick, and stay by the conditions of the marriage covenant or contract that we vowed to honor and uphold. Vows are to be kept—not broken. As a way of "sealing" their vows, one newly married couple went to the cemetery shortly after their wedding and purchased two burial plots. They were sending a powerful message to each other—for us, the relationship will end in death.

In today's society, too many have allowed the culture to shape and mold their view and definition of marital love and commitment. If there are not the "vibes," "feelings," and "emotions" that once existed, that's supposed to settle it. Divorce is the only alternative. The situation is totally beyond their control—they "fell into" love and now they have "fallen out of" love. For some, love has become an uncontrollable case of the "tingles." Where and when this is the case, commitment in marriage cannot exist and marital harmony is impossible. Strength of character and depth of commitment are always at the base of a home that can create beautiful harmony.

4. Our cultural and sub-cultural patterns clash.

Every bride and groom bring cultural and sub-cultural baggage into a marriage relationship. What is a culture? What are sub-cultures?

A **"culture"** is a discernable pattern of learned conduct, which tends to reflect the acceptable principles, patterns, preferences, pleasures, and priorities of one's daily environment. These learned patterns of daily life significantly affect the beliefs and behaviors of every individual.

"Sub-cultures" are distinct divisions and groups within the larger culture. These smaller sub-cultures have their own unique features and characteristics that distinguish them from other sub-cultures. For example, within the broad religious culture of American life, there are many sub-cultures made up of various religious groups that reflect distinct beliefs and behaviors.

All humans are impacted by the culture in which they live. They are affected at even deeper levels by their exposure to the sub-cultures of their daily lives. For example, a person's home of origin is a daily sub-culture. In some sub-cultures, the price at the meat market was a priority. In other sub-cultures, the price at the stock market was the main focus. These sub-cultural emphases can clash head-on in marriage. In some families of origin, hugging, kissing, and touching were common. In other clans, these behaviors were viewed as intrusive. In one setting, people yelled and openly expressed feelings and emotions when there was conflict. However, in other family settings, people grew up witnessing silent withdrawal and isolation when differences surfaced. One sub-culture may be socially, politically, and spiritually conservative. Another may embrace and teach views that are much more tolerant and liberal. It is a fact that our sub-cultures tend to have a powerful impact on the way we think, behave, relate, make decisions, play, worship, celebrate, and work.

Practices in one region of the country can clash with those in another region. Traditions can be very different. Literally, husbands and wives can be as far apart as "north and south" or "east and west." It is not uncommon to discover that people celebrate in different ways. What is socially acceptable in one setting may be considered morally unacceptable in another. Cooking styles in one family can be extremely different from the way other families prepare their food. What is acceptable in one local church may not be allowed in another. These differences and others can become hotspots for marriage partners. Blending our differences so as to create harmony rather than havoc is a challenge for many.

Individuals who were reared in the same culture-at-large may discover in marriage that they have radical differences due to the influences of their respective sub-cultures. It is no wonder that in the process of merging two lives in marriage, individuals can experience severe culture or sub-culture shock! You can marry a person who was reared in the house next door and still discover that the two of you have major differences, which can cause friction and fractures in the relationship.

Living In Harmony With One You Love Should Be Easy! But...

No wonder so many couples struggle with their matrimonial math— $1 + 1 = 1$! These numbers do not add up on a calculator and many are finding it difficult to make this formula work in marriage. There's nothing easy or simple about merging two lives into one loving relationship. But, with a deep commitment to the Lordship of Jesus Christ, harmony in the home can be experienced and enjoyed!

Harmony Building Exercises

1. In building a home with harmony, how essential is it for the husband and the wife to fully embrace the biblical truth that marriage is to last a lifetime? Give reasons for your answer.

2. Can you point to specific weaknesses in the modern day courting process? What new ideas or different methods related to courting would you like to implement when your children begin this process?

3. Do you agree or disagree with the assertion that no person can fully know the person he or she is marrying? How can the church contribute in a positive way toward healthy courting practices that prevent as many surprises as possible?

4. Based on your experience with the marriage merger, how would you rate the complexity of the process? Do you agree that marriage is one of life's most challenging mergers? What do you think about a "Marriage Mentoring" program that provides an avenue for younger couples to learn from older couples? (*Titus 2:1-5*)

5. It is true that poor role models can adversely affect the strength and stability of our marriages. However, this trend can be reversed. Can you share an example where you or someone you know has actually grown stronger because of a previous disappointment and failure? What can we do in God's church to turn this trend around and help people to learn from their negative experiences and never repeat destructive behaviors?

6. Share personal examples to illustrate how cultural and sub-cultural baggage has complicated your marriage merger. What helped you to resolve these clashes? What good counsel can you share with others who may be struggling to find a resolution to their differences at the present time?

7. Discuss the need for caution when tempted to put a spouse in a cultural or sub-cultural mold and assume things about him or her that may not be

accurate. Everyone is different and unique and must be dealt with in view of this truth. How hurtful and dangerous it can be to hastily say, "You are just like the rest of your family!"

8. As you read the following passages, look for biblical truths that, if applied, will enable us to have attitudes and take actions that will make the marriage merger easier.

    a. *1 Corinthians 13:4-8*

    b. *Romans 8:5-6*

    c. *Ephesians 4:2*

    d. *Ephesians 4:29*

    e. *Philippians 2:3-5*

9. Imagine four people singing in unison. Then, imagine four people singing in harmony. Which style is most touching and impressive to the human spirit? Why? How could we use this illustration to illustrate the power of "harmony in the home?"

CHAPTER 2
Sorting Out The "We" And "Me"—
Can There Be Harmony?

One Couple's Dilemma—How Many Candles Should Burn?

A Christian couple was thoughtfully planning their wedding ceremony. Both wanted to light a unity candle at the front of the church
building. Typically, in this part of the ceremony, there are two small
candles that burn to symbolize the two unique individuals that are
about to be joined in marriage. At the appropriate time, the bride
and groom use the two smaller candles to simultaneously light the
larger unity candle as a way of symbolizing their oneness as husband
and wife. After lighting the one unity candle, most couples extin-
guish the two smaller candles and put them back in place—one large
candle is left burning. The lighting and extinguishing of the candles
is supposed to convey an important message about the end of their
singleness and the beginning of their couple-ness.

This particular couple, however, wanted to slightly modify the
typical procedure. They would still use the two smaller candles to
light the larger unity candle. No change there. However, rather
than extinguishing the two smaller candles after the unity candle
was lighted; they opted to leave the two smaller candles burning at
each side of the larger unity candle. In the end, what the observer
saw was one large candle burning predominantly in the center and
two smaller candles burning on each side. In other words, all three
candles were left burning rather than one. Why the modification?
Simply because they wanted the symbolism of the candles to convey the clear message that while, first and foremost, they would be
"united partners" in marriage, they would also continue to be "unique
persons" created by God with very different gifts, creative abilities,
and distinct personalities. For them, leaving the three candles burning was a meaningful and healthy addition to the ceremony.

The "We" And "Me" Tension In Marriage

Marriage is a radical step that requires two single individuals to voluntarily give up freedom to think and act as totally independent persons—ever again. The marriage promise means that one deliberately chooses to be "out of circulation" and to eliminate the option of being married to anyone else. This is right. This is good. God's plan certainly calls for two to *"become one."*

But does this mean that each partner's unique identity, distinct personality, and creative gifts are to be sacrificed in the process? This can be a sensitive matter and create tensions if marital bonding begins to feel like marital bondage. One husband said, "I know God wants us to be one, but which one? In our blending, I am feeling like the one doing all of the bending!" The crux of the issue is, "In the process of becoming WE, what happens to ME?" Is there a way for us to enjoy a high level of couple-ness, while at the same time finding healthy and happy ways to preserve and exercise our individual God-given strengths and gifts? When this matter is not properly and lovingly resolved, deep-seated frustrations and resentments can set in.

Is This A Co-Dependency Issue?

Much has been written and said in recent years about the problem of co-dependency. Some of this counsel has steered people down a therapy path that is not conducive to building strong relationships in marriage. There is a co-dependency that is unhealthy and destructive, and there is a kind of marital co-dependency that is healthy and constructive. It all depends on how you define these terms.

Healthy co-dependency in marriage is where each partner behaves in such a way so as to facilitate and perpetuate Christian beauty, strength, attitudes, and behavior within the life of the other person. Her good is his greatest joy. His strength is her deepest desire. Instead of sucking the life out of each other, both are sincerely interested in the infusion of God's life, love, and light. Each partner contributes in a constructive way to the other person's physical, mental, emotional, social, and spiritual needs. When couples are co-dependent in this way, the words, "We need each other," mean that mutual respect, growth, and security are being fostered in each life. This is a healthy and constructive kind of co-dependency that should be encouraged and practiced by every married couple. When this dynamic is at work in the relationship, the quality of marital harmony is greatly enhanced.

On the other hand, unhealthy co-dependency occurs when the glue that holds two people together is their mutual brokenness and overwhelming neediness. The couple is caught in a web of woundedness, which tends to keep them weak and sickly. In these relationships, the words, "I need you," can mean "I need you to need me and I will keep you needy because, if you ever get better, you might leave me." The person believes that when his or her partner is no longer needy, he or she will have nothing to offer and end the relationship.

It is a black hole that sucks people into a spiral that is always downward. These unhealthy co-dependent relationships are sustained by manipulation and control. The environment is incredibly sick. If at one point, one partner was somewhat healthy, this contagious environment will cause him or her to set aside healthy values and ignore personal needs just to be close to someone who is in the process of self-destruction. It's called "enabling." Life is sucked out of both partners because their dysfunctional lives are so enmeshed.

Dealing With "We" And "Me"— Three Possible Approaches

1. A "sick dependency" in marriage weakens and destroys.

Where there is a sick kind of dependency in a marriage, there is no "me"—only "we." One marriage partner says to the other, "You must meet all of my needs." Neediness keeps them together. If this marriage were depicted graphically, there would be two circles placed on top of each other with almost no way to tell where one ends and the other begins. In this relationship, one's unique personality, creative abilities, and God-given skills are stifled or even totally sacrificed due to the insecurity of one or both partners. Separate interests, hobbies, or activities create a threat and tend to cause friction. Frequently, you will find that one partner is dominant and the other passive.

From a distance, such an enmeshment can look like intimacy, but it is not. Intimacy grows out of knowing each other very well, and being able to accept and love each other in spite of weaknesses and differences. Enmeshment is an attempt to think, feel, and act as if you were the same person.

This approach to marriage can lead to other complicating problems:

- A strong sense of possessiveness may exist—jealousy can be fueled and fed in this environment.
- A strong tendency to be controlling is common—one partner feeling that he or she has power over the other.
- This environment can foster physical and emotional abuse and violence.

2. A "selfish independency" in marriage separates and kills.

In this marriage, two people co-exist under the same roof, share the same mailing address, yet live a day-to-day existence as married singles. In this setting, there is very little "we-ness"—mostly a lonely and angry "me-ness." He goes his way. She goes her way. The most visible proof that this marriage even exists is a legal document called a marriage license on file at the courthouse. They are not together because of "warm love"—they stay together because of "cold law." They are "legally bound" but not "emotionally bonded." They don't "enjoy" their union—they only "endure it." Important matters are never discussed and the distance between them grows wider and wider.

If this marriage were depicted graphically, there would be two circles that barely touch—rarely is there much overlap. Daily communication consists primarily around facts and necessary details, but sadly the expression of feelings and needs is almost non-existent. Their relationship is like two fish bowls sitting side by side with a single fish in each tank. They can make a visual connection by long distance, but there can be no touching or togetherness. Living as married singles parallels the fish analogy. The husband and wife have physical proximity, yet there is a serious deficiency of emotional, physical, social, or spiritual intimacy.

This approach to marriage can lead to other complicating problems:

- Selfish independence in marriage on the part of one partner may generate deep resentment and harmful anger on the part of the neglected mate. They live in separate worlds and share no common love language.
- Depression and the loss of self-esteem on the part of one or both partners are inevitable.
- This environment leads to loneliness and is a seedbed for mental disease and physical health problems.

- In a situation where there is dissatisfaction with one's mate, the temptation to be unfaithful and commit sin can be increased.

3. A "satisfying interdependency" in marriage is a blessing to the home, the church, and the community-at-large.

A sick dependency is hurtful. A selfish independency is harmful. But a satisfying interdependency is helpful, healthy, and harmonious. How can this kind of relationship be described?

Satisfying interdependence in a marital relationship allows partners to move freely and comfortably between being both independent and dependent depending on the circumstances and conditions. Their marriage involves a contract of partnership—not ownership. It is an agreement to pursue common goals, while preserving a proper respect for each partner's unique personhood.

When there is healthy interdependence, the marriage partners love and cherish their sweet togetherness—their "we-ness"—but are also very comfortable allowing the other to experience an appropriate "me-ness." Without this necessary space in a marriage, femininity and masculinity cannot be fully experienced or enjoyed. She is free to be feminine and he is allowed to enjoy masculinity, while at the same time they find multiple ways to blend the two distinct mindsets into one harmonious partnership.

Someone might ask, "How much dependence and independence should be allowed in a relationship?" There can be no hard clad rules set forth as to how much individuality must be allowed or how many mutual interests a couple must share. One size does not fit all. Each couple is different and must work hard to find a healthy balance. If this marriage were depicted graphically, there would be two circles that are continually moving back and forth with varying amounts of overlap. In one setting, the two will be in complete overlap indicating a strong "we-ness," whereas in another setting the two circles may be very distinct indicating a state of individual independence and competency. Always, no matter what the situation, the two circles are touching. There is an abundance of "couple-time," but there is also "individual-time." Healthy couples learn complimentary ways of living and relating, which deepens intimacy and heightens harmony.

A warning is in order! "Me-ness" in marriage must never be expressed in a selfish, spiteful, or rebellious independence. Never should the pursuit of "me-ness" encourage self-centeredness. Bottom-line in marriage—"we" always has priority over "me." The "me" and "we" tension is lessened when marriage partners can live as close friends and companions as well as lovers. One happily married man said, "I don't just love my wife. I like her!" Obviously, the more a couple can share socially, emotionally, physically, culturally, and spiritually, the greater the opportunities for satisfying interdependence.

This approach to marriage blesses couples, benefits individuals, and strengthens the church.

- Healthy interdependence is mutually satisfying as "couple-needs" are met and "individual-needs" are not stifled.
- This approach to marriage enhances and deepens the respect that partners feel for each other. In this marriage climate, genuine compliments are given freely and frequently.
- In such marriages, the question is not, "What can I get from you?" but "What can I give to you and how can I receive from you so as to deepen our intimacy?" Each partner holds up his or her end of the relationship—neither end is left to drag.
- In this relationship, each person knows that he or she is loved, wanted, needed, protected, encouraged, and appreciated.

"He"..."Me"...And..."We"

Blending two selfish "me's"—a husband and wife—into one harmonious "we" is easier said than done. In the process of sewing two lives together, it's easy to rip the fabric. A mother put her son in the saddle of a mechanical horse at the local grocery store. Just behind him, she placed her young daughter telling the young lady to hold tightly to her brother. Riding conditions on the toy horse were cramped and crowded. In the middle of the ride, the brother turned around and said to his little sister, "If one of us would get off this horse, I would be more comfortable." Too often, in marriage, both partners are thinking, "If one of us would change, I would be so much happier." Is there a way to close the gaps and gradually achieve unity?

Jesus Christ can make the crucial difference! "He"—our Lord Jesus—must be the One who shows us the way out of our "selfish me-ness" into a "harmonious we-ness." When we, on our own, cannot seem to find acceptable connecting points in our backgrounds, cultures, customs, and personal preferences, there is still a way to find our way to each other in and through Him. This is not easy. It requires that both spouses be willing to walk with Jesus along the Calvary road. Having His loving and sacrificial spirit and attitude, we must be willing to "go to the Cross" for each other. When husbands live in the spirit of Calvary and when wives have the mindset that led Jesus to Golgotha, they can find harmony at the foot of the Cross. Marriage chasms that are deep and wide may separate us, but "He" can be the bridge that unites two "selfish me's" into one "Jesus-like we."

Harmony Building Exercises

1. Recall the scene described at the beginning of this chapter—the lighting of the unity candle. How do you view the significance of three burning candles vs. one burning candle at the end? Give reasons for your point of view.

2. In a marriage where there is too much detachment and distance between partners, there are many unmet personal needs. This generates frustration and anger. What other physical, emotional, and relational problems might surface in the lives of marriage partners whose partnership is filled with walls rather than bridges?

3. In this lesson, it was asserted that there can be a healthy kind of co-dependency in marriage. Share some ways that you and your spouse are co-dependent in a way that is mutually helpful and harmonious.

4. Jealousy can be a serious problem in marriage. At the same time, a cold indifference and lack of mutual concern can be just as serious. Discuss the parameters of a healthy and acceptable concern between marriage partners—one that is not rooted in a sick and sinful jealousy. How have you and your partner learned to relate in a caring way without perpetuating a dangerous kind of possessiveness?

5. Why is a marriage relationship so significant in the construction or destruction of a person's healthy self-esteem?

6. Married couples need lots of "couple-time." There is also a need for "individual-time." Do you agree with these statements? Share some of the ways that you and your spouse have been able to successfully achieve these goals.

7. It sounds good to say that "Jesus" is the bridge that unites two "selfish me's" into one "Jesus-like we." It's a good line, but can it really work? What

can we do to move Christian principles out of the realm of "theory" and into the daily arena of "practice" so that the gaps between us can be lessened and the problems be satisfactorily resolved?

8. In the creation of intimacy in marriage, do we ever "arrive?" Or, is the creation of intimacy something that requires continual work throughout the duration of marriage? Does the process get easier the longer we are married?

9. Would it be wise for marriage partners to say the following to each other: "No matter what the differences or difficulties, I will not leave you. I am committed to this relationship and will stay with you no matter what the circumstances?" Why would this be helpful? Could this be hurtful in any way?

10. In a healthy marriage where there is a strong sense of interdependence, what positive qualities and characteristics would you expect to see as you observe the couple interacting with each other?

11. Allow time for each participant to single out one passage in the Scriptures that could be applied in a helpful way to aid couples in sorting out the "me" and "we" tension in marriage.

CHAPTER 3

The Quest For Harmony In Marital Communication (Part 1)

Warning — Work Zone Ahead!

Learning to communicate in marriage is hard work. Applying good communication skills is not easy. Why? Because good communicators must learn to reveal their "below-the-surface-selves." This can be scary to the "revealer" and threatening to the "revealee." The former is afraid to say it and the latter is offended to hear it. Communication can be risky business. It can get messy—especially at the beginning of marriage. After one or two failed efforts, we decide we don't want to be that open and vulnerable with each other. Thus, we suppress our true feelings and bury all kinds of emotional junk inside of us, which clogs the flow of mutual trust, respect, and intimacy. A mountain of resentment, bitterness, and anger can get built up. Most of us need help in this area.

The ideal is when you have two willing participants who are eager to change old patterns and learn new skills. Will you agree to work with your partner and tackle some hard work in this crucial area? The next three lessons are devoted to the topic of marital communication. It's time to roll up our sleeves and go to work. Yes, there is risk involved, but the potential for a sweeter and more harmonious marriage is greatly enhanced. You are entering a "Work Zone."

HARMONY HEART WORK

❏ I need to be a better communicator with my spouse.

❏ I desire to be a better communicator with my spouse.

❏ I am willing to pray for strength to be a better communicator with my spouse.

❏ I am willing to admit that my attitude and actions have not always contributed to good communication with my spouse.

❏ I am willing to make an effort to improve communication with my spouse.

❏ I will open my heart and mind to new ideas and consider ways that I can improve as a communicator.

❏ I will agree to work hard to and make a good faith effort to improve as a communicator with my spouse.

Is Communication A Biblical Topic?

Is communication in marriage really a biblical topic? No doubt about it! The Bible contains many passages that relate directly or indirectly to the significance of communication. These principles can certainly be applied in the home setting. Here are just a few of the passages that illustrate the point.

He who guards his lips guards his life, but he who speaks rashly will come to ruin. (Proverbs 13:3)

A gentle answer turns away wrath, but a harsh word stirs up anger. . .The tongue that brings healing is a tree of life, but a deceitful tongue crushes the spirit. (Proverbs 15:1, 4)

A man finds joy in giving an apt reply—and how good is a timely word! The heart of the righteous weighs its answers, but the mouth of the wicked gushes evil. (Proverbs 15:23, 28)

Kings take pleasure in honest lips; they value a man who speaks the truth. . .The wise in heart are called discerning, and pleasant words promote instruction. . .A wise man's heart guides his mouth, and his lips promote instruction. Pleasant words are a honeycomb, sweet to the soul and healing to the bones. (Proverbs 16:13, 21, 23-24)

Ears that hear and eyes that see—the LORD has made them both. (Proverbs 20:12)

Therefore each of you must put off falsehood and speak truthfully to his neighbor, for we are all members of one body. "In your anger do not sin": Do not let the sun go down while you are still angry. . . Do not let any unwholesome talk come out of your mouths, but only what is helpful for building others up according to their needs, that it may benefit those who listen. (Ephesians 4:25-26, 29)

My dear brothers, take note of this: Everyone should be quick to listen, slow to speak and slow to become angry, for man's anger does not bring about the righteous life that God desires. . .If anyone considers himself religious and yet does not keep a tight rein on his tongue, he deceives himself and his religion is worthless. (*James 1:19-20, 26*)

We Are Communicating...But...

Just because two married people speak English is no guarantee that effective communication will occur between them. The key word in the previous sentence is "effective." Communication is always occurring, but too often it is not "effective." The fact is that you cannot...not communicate. Cold, dead silence is a form of communication even if the message is harmful and destructive. Ineffective communication in marriage will eventually take its toll and cause holy wedlock to become unholy deadlock. Most surveys indicate that poor marital communication ranks near the top of the list when it comes to major marriage killers.

Something's Not Right. We Just Can't Talk!

We learn to talk as toddlers, but something happens to many of us when we become marriage partners. Too often, we don't talk—at least not to each other about matters that are serious and significant. We may superficially express facts regarding weather, traffic, and work-related grievances, but rarely move to the deeper levels of our feelings, needs, struggles, and goals. The wheels of marriage are jammed and frozen by poor communication. Rather than being able to freely and openly discuss financial concerns, sexual needs, spiritual goals, moral struggles, family problems, or whatever, couples bury these matters and say nothing to each other. They live side by side in an emotionally solitary condition never really knowing what is in the heart of the other. In a healthy marriage, a husband and wife are able to give and receive communication on any subject.

We Must "Commune" In Order To "Communicate"

The dictionary defines the verb "to commune" as:

> **Commune**-"A state of intimate heightened sensitivity and receptivity that leads to the sharing of life; to get very close to someone or something by exchanging feelings or thoughts."

Marriage is to create a daily living environment in which a husband and wife learn "to commune" with each other. Note some of the key words in the definition cited above. When couples "commune," there is sensitivity. There is receptivity. There is a safe environment in which they are able to share their "below-the-surface-selves." When marriage partners "commune," there is a physical, emotional, and spiritual intimacy that encourages the honest sharing of feelings and thoughts. "Communion" is a "common-union." The point is that a couple must "commune" if there is to be "commune-ication."

The need to "commune" can be illustrated in other ways. For example, when Christians eat the Lord's Supper together, they "commune" with the Lord, which means they experience intimacy with Him as they thoughtfully share in His death, burial, and resurrection life. They also "commune" with each other as they eat "the one bread" and "drink the one cup." Sharing in this unity meal, believers in Christ are able to enjoy meaningful "commune-ion" or "common-union."

> *The cup of blessing which we bless, is it not the communion of the blood of Christ? The bread which we break, is it not the communion of the body of Christ? For we being many are one bread, and one body: for we are all partakers of that one bread. (1 Corinthians 10:16-17 KJV)*

There is another way to illustrate what it means "to commune." What is the term that we frequently use when people choose to live in close geographical proximity and are considered a social unit because of their common living space, interests, needs, and goals? This we call a "commune-ity.

The point should be clear. We must "commune"—share the fullness of our lives together in marriage—if we are to experience and enjoy the blessing of "commune-ication." A breakdown in "communication" is a sure sign that a couple is not "communing."

There Can Be High-Tech And Low Communication

One husband said to his wife, "I cannot believe what you are telling me! We have cell phones, home phones, high-speed internet access, computers, instant messaging, iPods®, digital Black Berries®, and webcams, yet you are telling me that we don't communicate!"

Communication in cyberspace and communication in marriage are two distinct realities. The former requires hardware and software. The latter requires hard work and soft hearts. You can be seconds away from a person on the other side of the globe, yet a world apart from your marriage mate who sits across the room.

Meaningful communication in marriage occurs when a husband and wife experience and enjoy a level of intimacy that allows them to deeply connect and commune with each other physically, mentally, emotionally, and spiritually. Slowly read those four areas again and consider the importance of each one. All four are important and essential in the quest for marital intimacy and harmony.

Take A Communication Tour Through Your "Marriage House"

Think of the large rectangle below as a diagram of . . . YOUR MARRIAGE HOUSE. This house has many rooms. Thus, take time to create various rooms in . . . YOUR MARRIAGE HOUSE . . . by drawing lines to serve as dividers. These rooms are to represent the many aspects and facets of your marriage relationship. (For example, write the word "God" in the center rectangle to indicate the central place of leadership that He should have. In the other spaces you create, write in "local church," "friends," "hobbies or interests," "finances," "job," "sex," "roles and responsibilities," "in-laws," "goals and dreams," "parenting," and any others that seem appropriate to represent your marriage relationship.)

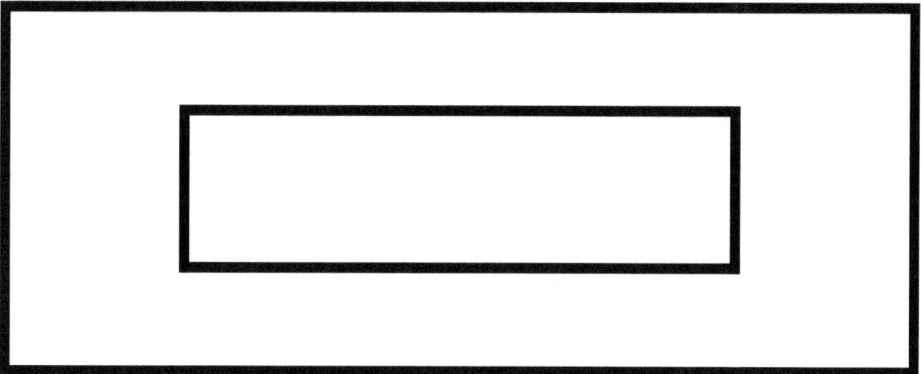

How Many "Rooms" Can You Experience Together?

Once you have divided the house into rooms and labeled each one, you are ready to ask yourself crucial questions. For example, how many rooms in YOUR MARRIAGE HOUSE can you enter with your spouse for constructive communication? Into how many of these spaces can you enter emotionally with your mate to openly and honestly discuss issues and feelings that relate to that particular area of married life? List below the rooms in YOUR MARRIAGE HOUSE that, from your vantage point, are partially or fully closed when it comes to open communication between you and your spouse. In a peaceful and prayerful spirit, compare your list with that of your spouse.

Partially Or Fully Closed Rooms In "Our Marriage House"

_____

_____

The "Ideal" Vs. "The Real"

Harmony in marriage is greatly enhanced when you are able to "enter every room" in YOUR MARRIAGE HOUSE with your spouse. When certain rooms seem to be closed off and partners are not able to connect in those marital spaces, communication blackouts occur. Frequently, it is in these areas of blackout that resentments and hostilities arise.

Once inside any of these spaces, you should be able to honestly share facts, opinions, feelings, needs, joys, desires, concerns, problems, hurts, and dreams, knowing that at the end of the discussion, there will still be mutual love, respect, and acceptance for each other. This is the IDEAL. Keep working hard to make it the REAL in your marriage. The goal, of course, is to keep all the rooms in YOUR MARRIAGE HOUSE open for mutual entry and open communication. And, when you discover closed spaces, resolve that you will work hard to re-open them.

What Blocks The Fuel Line Of Communication?

Just as it takes fuel to make cars go, it takes communication to make marriages work. When the fuel line of communication gets blocked or even clogged, couples begin to experience the "worse" part of that "for better or for worse" phrase in the wedding ceremony. What are some of the more common "blocks" to marital communication? After responding with honesty and humility to the leading statements below, share your insights with your mate. The goal of this exercise is to unclog the lines that fuel meaningful and helpful communication in your marriage.

1. Guard against "the daily drift."

Neither marriage partner desires it or maliciously plots to make it happen. It's just a gradual daily drift that takes its toll over time on the relationship. All couples must deal with it—the everyday stuff of life—busyness, financial pressures, job stressors, children, conflict, fatigue, or any other factor that puts emotional distance between you and your marriage mate. One day you look across the table and see a person that you no longer know. Guard against "the daily drift."

> One specific thing I can do to prevent "the daily drift" in my marriage is to
>
> _____
>
> _____

2. Beware of "walls of bitterness."

Harbored hurts and wounded spirits block communication. Feelings are delicate. They get hurt easily. Even if you feel the offense was not intended and the hurt is totally unjustified, the hard truth is that emotional walls can get erected quickly and communication shuts down. Do you know your marriage partner so well that you can identify certain behaviors that are likely to offend and adversely affect communication?

> I have learned from experience that I am likely to emotionally hurt my spouse and adversely affect our efforts to communicate when I
>
> _____
>
> _____

3. Address "the fear factor."

When "the fear-factor" is at work in a marriage, a spouse will say, "I need to talk to my mate. I want to share my feelings and needs. But, I am afraid. I don't like conflict. I have tried in the past to broach certain issues, but nothing was resolved. If anything, the situation worsened. I have decided that talking about it won't do any good. I don't think I can bring these matters up ever again." This attitude is rooted in fear and communication is blocked.

> I know that I tend to stifle communication and create fear within my spouse when I
>
> _____
>
> _____

4. Change the "adversarial climate."

Where there is closeness in a human relationship, there is likely to be some conflict. Some frustration and anger are perfectly normal in marriage. What is not healthy or helpful is an atmosphere where there is continual hostility, attacks, and counter-attacks. When a couple lives in an environment where there is impatience, negativity, sarcasm, criticism, and arguing, effective communication is made impossible.

> One thing that I can do to lessen the adversarial climate in my marriage and create an atmosphere that will be more conducive to good communication is
>
> _____
>
> _____

5. Change the "my partner just knows assumption."

Some marriage partners embrace the myth that "true love just knows." It is a mistake to assume that your partner knows what you are thinking or feeling and thus will provide 100% affirmation. How presumptuous and naïve! This is a sure set-up for a letdown. This "love me so truly and know me so deeply so that I don't have to talk to you" is a daydream that leads to a nightmare in marriage. Feelings get hurt and conflict occurs when we do not clearly transmit the messages that we want our partners to receive. Don't operate on the false premise that you and your marriage mate are so close that he or she will know what you need. Don't expect heavy affirmation when you have given only light communication.

Whatever the desire, the feeling, or the need, we must find appropriate ways to clearly communicate with our partners.

One specific area where I have failed to clearly communicate my desires, feelings, and needs with my mate is

_____

_____

Knowing that my mate cannot read my mind and automatically provide the affirmation that I need, I resolve to

_____

_____

6. Watch out for "communication avoidance habits."

It can be subtle. You may not even see it happening. We can find ways to avoid serious conversations with our mates. For example, by staying so busy, we don't have time to sit down and communicate about important matters. If you work long hours at the office or shop, there is no time left to talk. Or, if you are so covered up with activities related to your hobbies and personal projects, there is little time to converse with a mate. Going out with another couple or always choosing to socialize in a group setting can be escape routes to keep us from having to talk with each other. Watching TV or spending time on-line can be subtle avenues of escape. Even "church work" can keep us so occupied that there is no time for communication.

It is possible that I avoid opportunities for communication by

_____

_____

Harmony Building Exercises

1. Check the statement below that comes closest to reflecting your feeling when it comes to the communication that is presently occurring in your marriage.

    ☐ From my vantage point, the quality of marital communication in my marriage is high. My spouse and I have learned to share facts, opinions, feelings, and needs with a spirit of honesty, openness, and mutual respect.

    ☐ From my vantage point, marital communication is moderately difficult. My spouse and I struggle in this area at times, but I feel encouraged because both of us are willing to learn and grow in this area.

    ☐ From my vantage point, marital communication is a frequent struggle. My spouse and I are finding it difficult to communicate about important matters without arguing.

2. Look over all the biblical passages that appear in this lesson. As you think about yourself and the constructive changes that you need to make as a communicator in marriage, select one passage that addresses a specific need that you have as a communicator with your spouse. Be prepared to share why the principles in this passage would improve your efforts as a communicator.

3. Identify a Christian couple that, from your vantage point, really seems "to commune" with each other. What do you see in their relationship that leads you to believe there is a meaningful and rewarding "communion" between them?

4. Based on your personal experience at home, how would you evaluate the overall effect that modern technology is having on your marriage and family? Is technology enhancing the relationship in specific ways and improving communication in the marriage and family?

5. In this chapter, six "blocks" to marital communication were mentioned—the daily drift, walls of bitterness, the fear factor, an adversarial climate, the "my partner just knows" assumption, and communication avoidance habits. Can you identify other "blocks" that hinder communion and communication in marriage?

6. In surveys that are taken across the land, why do you suppose many couples identify "communication" as the crucial area that seems to have the greatest impact on all other aspects of marriage? Do you agree or disagree with that assessment? Why?

CHAPTER 4
The Quest For Harmony In Marital Communication (Part 2)

It Takes "The Parts" And "A Partnership"

Most of us have the physical body parts to make verbal communication happen—a brain, a tongue, lips, eyes, ears, vocal cords, and a vocabulary. Even with this equipment in place, we frequently feel poorly equipped to communicate effectively with our marriage partners. Could it be that while we have "the physical parts," we lack "the emotional partnership" necessary to create an environment of trust, respect, and intimacy? Learning new verbal techniques, listening skills, and conflict therapy is an exercise in futility unless there is a genuine desire for heart-level communication. Coming out of a marital communication seminar, one man said to his wife, "Now that we have learned to communicate, shut up!" The "part" of marital communication that matters the most is "the partnership."

Communication—It's Verbal And Non-Verbal

All sorts of cues are part of the communication process. Messages are constantly being sent through two important channels—verbal and non-verbal. Communication research tells us that approximately 45% of our communication is verbal and 55% is non-verbal. What an amazing fact! We actually convey more non-verbally than we do with our words. In this chapter we will explore some of the factors that affect our efforts to connect verbally and non-verbally with our marriage partners.

What Is Happening When We Attempt To Communicate?

Communication is a complex two-way process. A basic understanding of the overall process is important if we are to learn new communication skills or improve present communication abilities. So, what is happening when a husband and wife are attempting to communicate with each other?

The primary goal of marital communication is mutual understanding—not agreement. This is a key point. Agreement between two people is wonderful, but not essential to communication. What is absolutely essential is that we are able to understand each other. Understanding is the meat and potatoes of the communication process. Agreement is the apple pie and vanilla ice cream that adds a marvelous final touch.

Below, you will find a graphic that illustrates the dynamics that occur in a communication setting. **On the next page there are written explanations (see numbers in shaded boxes) that correspond to the numbers in the graphic itself.** By connecting the written explanations with the images in the drawing, you will catch a glimpse of "THE BIG PICTURE" of what is happening when husbands and wives share facts and feelings with each other as they attempt to communicate.

DYNAMICS OF COMMUNICATION

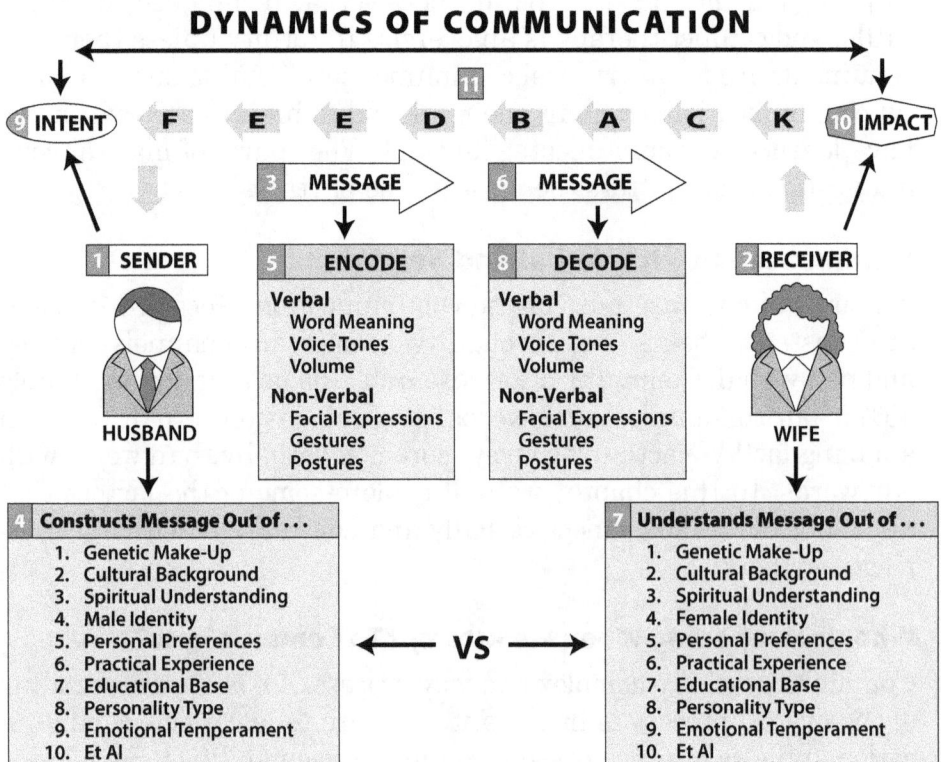

9 INTENT F E E D B A C K **10 IMPACT**

11

3 MESSAGE **6 MESSAGE**

1 SENDER

5 ENCODE

Verbal
  Word Meaning
  Voice Tones
  Volume

Non-Verbal
  Facial Expressions
  Gestures
  Postures

HUSBAND

8 DECODE

Verbal
  Word Meaning
  Voice Tones
  Volume

Non-Verbal
  Facial Expressions
  Gestures
  Postures

WIFE

2 RECEIVER

4 Constructs Message Out of . . .

1. Genetic Make-Up
2. Cultural Background
3. Spiritual Understanding
4. Male Identity
5. Personal Preferences
6. Practical Experience
7. Educational Base
8. Personality Type
9. Emotional Temperament
10. Et Al

VS

7 Understands Message Out of . . .

1. Genetic Make-Up
2. Cultural Background
3. Spiritual Understanding
4. Female Identity
5. Personal Preferences
6. Practical Experience
7. Educational Base
8. Personality Type
9. Emotional Temperament
10. Et Al

A Written Explanation Of The Graphic On the Opposite Page:

1. For communication to occur there must be a sender. Locate the SENDER-HUSBAND in the graphic above.

2. For communication to occur there must be a receiver. Locate the RECEIVER-WIFE on the graphic.

3. In this graphic, the sender-husband desires to send a MESSAGE to his receiver-wife. (See #3). The ideal is for this message to reveal accurate facts, honest thoughts, true feelings, and deep needs. In the upper left corner of the graphic, note figure #9. This is "the shape" that represents what the husband "intends" to convey to his wife. Will he be able to help his wife understand his intent?

4. Before the message can be sent, it must be CONSTRUCTED. How is this done? The sender-husband builds his message by drawing from deep within himself. He digs into many resources that are unique to him as a person. Some of these resources are listed in the box. Study these factors carefully.

5. Once the husband knows what he wishes to say to his wife, the message must now be ENCODED for transmission. This occurs when the sender-husband selects VERBAL and NON-VERBAL SIGNALS to use for his transmission. The verbal part of his communication is affected by such things as WORD MEANINGS, VOICE TONES, and VOLUME. The non-verbal portion of his communication is conveyed by such things as FACIAL EXPRESSIONS, GESTURES, and POSTURE.

6. The encoded message is SENT to the receiver-wife.

7. The receiver-wife listens to the message from her sender-husband. As she listens, she must attempt to UNDERSTAND the message. How does she do this? She seeks to interpret and understand his message by drawing from within herself. She digs deep into the unique resources that make her the person she is. Obviously, her foundational resources are very different from those of her husband. Do these foundational differences between the husband and wife affect understanding in the communication process? How? Why?

8. In the process of trying to understand her husband's message, she must DECODE it. That is, she must begin to actually attach meanings to the verbal and non-verbal messages she has received.

9.
10. The message has now been sent, received, and processed. Note the shape of the HUSBAND'S INTENT. (See #9 at top left.) Note the shape of the WIFE'S IMPACT—her interpretation and understanding of his message. (See #10 at top right.) The painful reality is that what he wanted to say (#9) is not precisely what she heard (#10). Mis-communication between the two has occurred to some degree. HIS INTENT does not equal HER IMPACT. What happens next depends on the desire and willingness of the couple to keep on working at their communication efforts. If the mis-communication between them creates bitterness and anger, which causes the couple to slam the door on each other, the relationship will suffer. A communication shutdown—temporarily or permanently—occurs. However, if the couple is willing to keep on working at communication, they may be able to gradually close the "understanding gap" by moving to the next important part of the process.

11. Once the couple determines that their goal of mutual understanding has not been achieved, then the whole process must be reversed. The wife becomes "the sender" and the husband becomes "the receiver." The sender-wife re-phrases and re-sends the message back to the receiver-husband. This second exchange of ideas, feelings, desires, and needs is called FEED-BACK. Ideally, the process continues back and forth until there is a message upon which they can share understanding or possibly even agreement.

A Closer Look At The Verbal Channel Of Communication

The crucial factor in verbal communication is not what you thought you said or even what you actually said. What really counts is what your mate heard you say. Verbal communication can be much more complex than we realize, as illustrated below.

1. Word meanings can result in misunderstanding.

Words are merely symbols that mean nothing except by mutual agreement between the sender and the receiver. For example, the word "elephant" refers to a huge thick-skinned, four-footed mammal with a long, flexible snout because this is the meaning that we have given to the word "elephant." So long as the sender and receiver share mutual meanings of the words that are exchanged, the opportunity for clear communication is enhanced.

The difficulty comes when we use words that can have more than one meaning. His definition may not be her definition. For example, what conclusion would you reach if you heard me say, "I beat my wife up every morning?" One person could legitimately conclude that I treat my wife violently every morning. The message I actually intended to send was that it is my practice to get out of bed before my wife every morning. The same words are used, but two very different messages are heard. Different word meanings can alter the messages that we send to another person.

2. Voice emphasis can change the meaning entirely.

It's not just what you say, but how you say it. So often we speak to our mates and fail to understand that volume, inflection, and voice emphasis can seriously change the message we want to convey. For example, try this exercise with a degree of exaggeration in your voice in order to emphasize the point being made. Below, you will find a sentence that contains seven words. Repeat the sentence aloud seven times giving heavy emphasis to the word that appears in bold print. By putting strong emphasis on the different words in the sentence, you will discover that the meaning will change seven times. Try it.

I didn't say your mother was stupid.

I *didn't* say your mother was stupid.

I didn't *say* your mother was stupid.

I didn't say *your* mother was stupid.

I didn't say your *mother* was stupid.

I didn't say your mother *was* stupid.

I didn't say your mother was *stupid*.

Get the point? How many times do we send messages that stir anger and block communication by the way we emphasize certain words? Communication is not simple or easy.

3. Your tone over-rides your words.

Researchers tell us that of the 45% of our communication that utilizes sound waves, only 7% of our message is conveyed by the actual words we speak. This is amazing! This means that 38% of the message we are transmitting with the use of sound, is conveyed to others by the tones we use. The tone is more crucial than the actual words we speak.

Words convey information and facts. Tones convey feelings and emotions. Before you have finished your first sentence in a verbal exchange, your spouse knows your attitude by the tone of your voice. When your words say one thing and your tone of voice says the opposite, guess which message your partner is likely to hear? You may use pleasing words on the surface, but if the tone surrounding those words sends a very different message, clear communication is blocked.

Using different "tone sounds," send the following messages with the little expletive "Hmm."

Send The Message Of...*Anger*

Send The Message Of...*Doubt*

Send The Message Of...*Surprise*

Send The Message Of...*Sadness*

Send The Message Of...*Pleasure*

Send The Message Of...*Indifference*

Send The Message Of...*Pain*

The Tone Of The Voice
(Author Unknown)

It's not so much what you say
As the manner in which you say it;
As the tone in which you convey it.
"COME HERE!" I said sharply.
And the child cowered and wept.
"Come here," I said tenderly.
And the child looked at me, smiled,
And to my lap he crept.

A Closer Look At The Non-Verbal Channel Of Communication

Some communication researchers tell us that a staggering 55% of what we communicate to others is conveyed by the non-verbal messages we send. This means that the majority of what people perceive about us and receive from us is based on appearance, posture, facial expressions, body language, touch, eye motion, and gestures. In the following exercise, visualize the non-verbal posture or gesture being described and then write the message that this would convey to you.

NON-VERBAL COMMUNICATION

You are having a serious talk with your mate. He or she keeps yawning while you are speaking and staring off into space. The message is...

_____

_____

You are speaking with your mate. There is disagreement and conflict. While you are attempting to convey your feelings about the matter, your mate rolls his or her eyes in an upward direction and wears a facial smirk. The message is...

_____

_____

You and your marriage partner go to bed in total silence. Your backs are to each other as you cling to the extreme east and west sides of the mattress. The message is...

_____

_____

Three days after a major argument, one marriage partner is still not speaking. The message is...

_____

_____

A partner in the marriage refuses to practice good hygiene, show any concern for his or her physical appearance, or use good manners. The message is...

_____

_____

In the midst of a discussion pertaining to finances, a marriage partner suddenly gets up, walks out, and slams the door. The message is...

_____

_____

Harmony Building Exercises

1. In this chapter, the point was made that, while agreement between a husband and wife is wonderful, it is not absolutely essential in order to have good communication. Do you agree with this statement? How would you describe a couple that cannot co-exist in peace and harmony until they are totally agreed on all points of contention?

2. When marriage partners are in the middle of a serious discussion, why is it so difficult to practice the guidelines described in this chapter—guidelines that would enable us to practice effective communication techniques? What prompts us to break these rules?

3. Read _John 3:1-8_. In this conversation between Jesus and Nicodemus, there is a great example to illustrate how word meanings can affect communication. Discuss this passage in light of what has been studied.

4. In the list below, place a check mark beside the attitudes and behaviors that would not occur if marriage partners applied the principles described in _Colossians 3:8_.

- ☐ Honest and open discussion
- ☐ Ugly name calling
- ☐ Silence and pouting
- ☐ Agree to disagree
- ☐ Yelling
- ☐ Disagreement
- ☐ Cursing
- ☐ A seven day grudge

5. How something is said is very important. What principle do you see in *Colossians 4:6* that confirms this truth?

6. Of all the helpful points covered in this lesson on martial communication, which one do you feel you needed the most?

CHAPTER 5
The Quest For Harmony In Marital Communication (Part 3)

Ears Are Beautiful!

We don't ordinarily think of ears as beautiful parts of the body. They never get featured on the covers of magazines. There are not many songs or poems about ears. No one seems to compliment them. When did anyone come to you and say, "Nice set of ears you've got!" In fact, ears take lots of abuse. They get twisted by parents, punctured by metal shafts, invaded by gnats, clogged by wax, burned by the sun, frozen by the cold, and assaulted by a variety of loud noises. Some even get nibbled on now and then.

The truth is that ears are the marvelous creation of God. They are beautiful and the ability to hear is one of God's most precious gifts.

He who answers before listening—that is his folly and shame. . . The heart of the discerning acquires knowledge; the ears of the wise seek it out. (Proverbs 18:13, 15)

My dear brothers, take note of this: Everyone should be quick to listen, slow to speak and slow to become angry,...(James 1:19)

He who has ears to hear, let him hear. (Matthew 11:15)

Do you have ears but fail to hear? (Mark 8:18)

Are We Using Our Ears To Listen To Each Other?

The need to be heard and understood is a fundamental human need. This is certainly true in marriage. In the midst of marital conflict, how often do husbands and wives say the following?

- You're not listening to me!
- Will you let me finish what I am saying?
- I might as well be talking to a log.

- That is not what I said!
- What I say to you goes in one ear and out the other.
- I think you need to get your hearing checked.

Find a husband who is happily married and he will say of his wife, "She listens to me." Find a wife who is truly happy with her husband and she will say, "I can talk to him." Those who are unhappy will say just the opposite. Talking is only one part of the communication process. Listening is the other essential part. If one of you is talking and the other is not listening, you are not communicating. When you truly listen to another person, you seek to understand what is being said and felt.

In the previous chapter, our focus was on "sending skills." In this chapter, the emphasis will be "receiving skills."

Listening—Before And After Marriage

Let your mind drift back to those courting days when your relationship was fresh and exciting. You had so much in common. You could finish each other's sentences. You were in sync. You couldn't wait to be together and everything that you said to each other was important. You listened and you felt listened to. In fact, talking and listening to each other were major factors in bringing the two of you together. You loved to sit close and look into each other's eyes. You hung on each other's words.

What happens to so many couples after the marriage knot is tied? The same two people who once enjoyed talking and listening can now barely get through to each other.

It should be pointed out that there is a natural ebb and flow even in good marriages. Marriages have peaks and valleys and we must be prepared to handle both. There are days of frustration, boredom, and anger. There are those times when listening is difficult. A growing marriage has predictable periods of down-ness and we should accept them as healthy and normal. No realistic person expects to live on the emotional high that may have existed during some of those dating days. With the advent of jobs, chores, finances, children, conflicts, bad breath, snoring, nagging, stubbornness, and other such realities, the everydayness of life tends to set in. During these times, the music of marriage is not so harmonious. In fact, it is badly off-key!

Through these normal ups and downs, couples must continue to work at communicating effectively as they live together in the close quarters of marriage. Our marriage music must not stay off-key. Harmony must be restored. Keeping the lines of communication up and open after marriage is a continual challenge for every couple. Even though the relationship is different from the courting days, the necessity of staying in close touch and communicating effectively must not change. This is essential if we are to keep our marriages strong.

What Is Happening In This Marriage?

Below, you will be reading a conversation between a husband and wife. After reading their conversation, use the space provided to list some of the major problems that you feel are hindering their relationship and efforts to communicate.

A Husband-Wife Conversation

She: Hi, honey. Would you be willing to work with me in finding some time for us? It just seems like life is so busy and we have little time or no time to connect with one another the way we once did. I miss those good times of sharing with you and really knowing where you are.

He: Yeah, I know we need to do this—it's just that I am under pressure at work and am trying to spend any extra time that I have with the kids. I don't want to neglect them. But, I promise, we'll try to find some time to be together real soon. Remind me again, if you will.

She: I know. That's what you've said in the past. I am feeling like it may never happen. We keep talking about it, but it never happens.

He: No, this time I am serious. We will get together. I know this is important to you and I plan to work it out. But, please don't pressure me about it. I don't need any more of a load than I already have.

She: I don't understand. When we were courting, you would sit and talk to me for hours. You were so willing and so receptive. You would share your dreams and goals. You would even tell me about your needs, fears, and hurts. We were so close. Don't you remember how we would sit up half the night holding each other and talk about our future together? Now, we never share anything like this. We never share our feelings or needs any more. I am hurting!

He: I don't know how you can say these things. Don't you see that we talk all the time? We still have conversations with each other. You can tell me anything you please.

She: Yes, we talk, but we never talk at a deeper level. Our talk is very superficial. We touch on things like which bills to pay, serious problems in the world, and when the children and I will make another trip to visit my folks. Yes, we talk, but we don't communicate.

He: Well, I think you are making a mountain out of a molehill. I think everything is just fine the way it is.

What major problems do you see in this marriage?

Problem #1:_____

Problem #2:_____

Problem #3:_____

Problem #4:_____

Problem #5:_____

A "Hearing Problem" Or A "Listening Problem?"

How well do you hear?

How well do you listen?

Are these the same questions? ❑ Yes ❑ No

Explain your answer.

Hearing and listening are very different experiences. You can have excellent hearing, yet be a very poor listener. Hearing is the reception of sound. This phenomenon can be explained by science. Listening is the apprehension and comprehension of verbal and non-verbal signals and sounds. Science alone cannot explain what happens when someone truly listens.

Fundamental to good listening is the willingness to consider each other's point of view. Such willingness is rooted in mutual respect and trust. Two marriage partners can say and even understand an endless flow of words back and forth between them. But, unless each cares enough about what the other is saying and about what his or her own words mean to the other, communication will not occur, except perhaps on the surface level. Caring about what another person says, thinks, and feels is tantamount to truly caring for that person. Listening carefully to another person is one of the highest compliments you can give.

Jesus Was A Good Listener

Our Lord was tuned in to the people around Him. He heard their cries for help, for forgiveness, and for guidance. His ears were sensitive to such sounds. The cry of one lone beggar in the crowded streets of Jericho was enough to stop Him in His tracks. The unspoken cry of a little man who climbed a sycamore tree prompted Jesus to look up and say, *"Zacchaeus, come down immediately. I must stay at your house today."* (*Luke 19:5*) When a woman named Mary came to a banquet Jesus was attending and poured expensive perfume on His feet, she was speaking eloquently, though not with words. Some in the room interpreted her message as wastefulness. Jesus heard the message of her heart and received her gift as an expression of love. Even on the cross, His ears were quick to hear the cry of the struggling man who said, *"Jesus, remember me when you come into your kingdom."* (*Luke 23:42*)

Guidelines For Practicing Good Listening Skills

While it is true that many people don't feel listened to, it is also true that most of us do not listen very well. In a very real sense, listening is a Christian ministry. We actually need to work hard at becoming listening specialists. Here are some guidelines that will help us to be better listeners as we relate to our mates and others in the family.

1. Work at being an open and available person.

Take down the "Do Not Disturb" sign you have been wearing. When you are too busy to listen to a spouse or to others in your family, you are too busy! Pay attention when your attitude says to others, "Get lost. I don't care!"

2. Don't do all the talking.

You cannot listen when you are talking. If you rearrange the letters in the word "listen," you have the word...S-I-L-E-N-T. In order to listen, we must remain silent. If it's "all about you," the relationship will suffer and communication breaks down.

3. Cultivate a genuine desire to understand what your mate or other family member is saying to you.

Get your antennas out! Be like a vacuum cleaner—an active listener—rather than a funnel—a passive listener. Care so deeply about the other person that you want to know what he or she is saying and feeling.

4. Get rid of distractions.

Concentration is essential. You cannot listen and be multi-tasking. Put down the paper. Turn off the TV. Shut down the computer. Get off the phone. Make the family member you are listening to the number one priority. Make sure you are "in the moment" emotionally. Good listening requires undivided attention.

5. Listen with your heart as well as your ears.

Make a genuine effort to see the situation through the other person's eyes. Focus on "intent" as well as "content." Listen for feelings as well as facts. The facial expression, the stance, the gestures, the pauses and hesitations may tell you more about the real message than the words you are hearing. Listen with a desire to get inside the skin of the loved one speaking to you. *"Rejoice with those who rejoice and mourn with those who mourn." (Romans 12:15)* The instruction of this passage is not to cheer up the person who mourns, but to share in the grief being experienced.

6. Do not try to listen while at the same time you are preparing your defense or response.

We do poor listening when we concentrate on the response we want to give rather than concentrating on the message we are receiving.

7. Avoid interruptions and allow the person to say what he or she wishes to say.

Part of honoring a person with the gift of listening is to let them finish their thoughts before giving your thoughts. Don't assume that you already know what they will say. Once you have listened to their thoughts, then respond thoughtfully. Politely take turns as you dialogue with your spouse.

8. Be aware of your body language as you listen.

Eye contact is important in good listening. Charles Spurgeon said, "It is an annoyance if even a blind man does not look me in the face." If you are fidgeting, staring off into space, or preoccupied with something or someone else, the message you send is that you are either not listening or don't care.

9. Ask questions, encourage elaboration, and give feedback.

A good listener will ask questions. This should be done to facilitate understanding and encourage sharing—not to criticize or ridicule. "Tell me more," encourages the speaker. "What happened next?" or "How did that make you feel?" are the questions of an eager listener. Feedback is crucial in communication. After a few sentences into a serious conversation, say, "Let me see if I am understanding you." One wife tells of a practice used by her husband. He would stop her in the middle of a quarrel and say, "What am I saying and what are you saying, and what's the difference?" She indicated that this practice is infuriating but effective in closing communication gaps.

10. Listening is most difficult when strong emotions and deep feelings are involved.

Patience in listening is hardest to do when you feel hurt, angry, sad, rejected, bitter, lonely, and not understood. Yet good listening counts the most when it is hardest to do. When emotions are running high, the strong tendency is to tune out the speaker, become defensive, attack, or want to give advice. We all prefer to listen when what is being said pleases us and we find it easy to reject anything that calls for a change of belief or behavior on our part.

Learning To Practice Open Listening

Your response as a listener can have the effect of keeping a channel of communication open or shutting it down. A comment, a look, a gesture, or even a grunt can cause another person to quit talking.

The goal of a good communicator is to encourage meaningful conversation between loved ones.

In the illustration below, you will see a contrast between "closed listening" and "open listening." Christian love calls for us to practice open listening as we relate to each other.

Open Communication

Family Statements	What is the Feeling?	A Closed Response	An Open Response
Wife: *"Honey, sometimes you look so angry that I want to be away from you."*	**Fear**	**Husband:** *"There's the door! Leave!"*	**Husband:** *"My anger is a problem, I know. Let's talk and work on it together."*
Husband: *"We never seem to have much time together. We are spending all of our time working."*	**Lonely Isolated**	**Wife:** *"I guess all you know how to do is gripe!"*	**Wife:** *"Honey, you really are needing some time for us to spend together aren't you?"*
Child: *"None of the kids at school will play with me. They just tell me to leave."*	**Hurt Rejected**	**Parent:** *"You need to quit being such a baby!"*	**Parent:** *"You are feeling hurt and rejected aren't you? We need to talk about it, don't we?"*
Wife: *"Staying at home all the time with the kids is rough. I sometimes need a break."*	**Pressure Stress**	**Husband:** *"You ought to have to do what I do every day. Your job is a breeze!"*	**Husband:** *"You are feeling some fatigue and need a change of pace aren't you? Let's talk."*

Harmony Building Exercises

1. Rate your own listening skills by circling the number below that represents how well you are performing at the present time.

	Inadequate						Adequate			
My desire to listen carefully	1	2	3	4	5	6	7	8	9	10
Not interrupting my mate	1	2	3	4	5	6	7	8	9	10
Being open and available	1	2	3	4	5	6	7	8	9	10
Willingness to hear another view	1	2	3	4	5	6	7	8	9	10
Not multitasking while listening	1	2	3	4	5	6	7	8	9	10
Listening with heart and ears	1	2	3	4	5	6	7	8	9	10
Listening with good body language	1	2	3	4	5	6	7	8	9	10
Asking questions	1	2	3	4	5	6	7	8	9	10
Not closing ears due to emotions	1	2	3	4	5	6	7	8	9	10
Planning a response—not listening	1	2	3	4	5	6	7	8	9	10
Skill in practicing open listening	1	2	3	4	5	6	7	8	9	10

Determine your overall listening score by adding together your "11" circled responses. My total score is: _____

Once you have your total score, divide this number by "11." This number represents your overall "Listening Score." My overall listening score is _____

How to rate your "Overall Listening Score."

> *The number "1" represents a "poor listener."*
>
> *The number "10" signifies a "perfect listener."*
>
> *Where are you?*

CHAPTER 6
Marital Finances—Harmony Or Harm?

"The Knot" And "The Purse Strings"

Once the "marital knot" is tied, then comes the hard work of making sure the purse strings don't get knotty. Chances are that money-related issues tend to spark some of the disputes that you have with "your spendthrift, tightfisted, financially clueless, or controlling spouse." Any combination of "financial personalities" in a marriage can lead to controversy over money. For example, two big spenders can dig a deep hole of debt. One big spender and one big saver can build a high wall of resentment and anger. And, even where you have two big savers, there can be a logjam of disagreement over how much to save and where to put it.

With the best of intentions, we repeated that marriage vow, "I take you to be my partner for life—for richer or for poorer." These words sound sweet during the wedding ceremony, but later, if the "for poorer" days begin to greatly out number the "for richer" days, those sweet words can turn into bitter feelings. Instead of experiencing marital harmony, it can feel more like marital harm. Even marriages that we would classify as seasoned and successful will, at times, experience episodes of stress and strife over finances.

Family Finances And The Impact Of Culture

We live in a culture of super markets, super malls, and super sales. Shopping opportunities on-line and otherwise are available to us 24/7. The spirit of consumerism is in the air that we breathe. The desire to buy is strong and advertisers know how to keep those fires fueled. The problem is not new. Adam and Eve had everything in the Garden of Eden except for one tree. Yet, guess what they wanted?

Our desire for stuff is very strong. We are attracted, distracted, gripped, owned, tempted and seduced by it. Could it be that our need and desire for stuff consumes more of our waking moments than our desire for God? Perhaps this explains why the Holy Spirit spoke so frequently about money and greed in the Scriptures.

HARMONY HEART WORK

As painful as it may be to admit, it is likely that many of our money-related problems are spiritual in nature. Read the passages listed below and use the spaces provided to give a brief summary of each one. You should be looking for biblical principles that will influence your thinking and practice when it comes to how money is to be viewed, made, and used by Christians. Remember that problems of the heart are not solved with calculators.

Deuteronomy 8:17-18...

_____

_____

1 Timothy 6:6-10...

_____

_____

Luke 12:13-21...

_____

_____

Luke 12:22-31...

_____

_____

1 Timothy 6:17-19...

_____

_____

Philippians 4:11-13...

_____

_____

2 Corinthians 9:6-8...

_____

_____

Me—Into Consumerism? Us—Materialistic?

Is it possible that we are so enmeshed in the consumerism and materialism of our day that we don't even see how they are affecting our lives? Could we be like fish that don't sense the water around them? One major hitch is that the affluent American culture views consumerism and stuff as part and parcel of normal living. This is just "the way it is." How can that be wrong?

Consumerism is the spirit that keeps us always wanting something else no matter what we just purchased or how much we already own. How can we measure the spirit of consumerism that is influencing our lives? To what extent are we guilty of the sin of materialism? The questions listed below may provide some insight that will help us discover how pervasive these forces are in our individual lives and marriages.

HARMONY HEART WORK

1. How much margin is there in your life? Do you have free time? Do you have free money? Are you so busy that there is little if any time left to serve others? Could it be that a craving for stuff is taking its toll on your spiritual focus and energy?

   Read the parable recorded in *Luke 8:4-15*. What is the meaning of verse 14?

   _____

   _____

2. Do you live below your income? Are you able to pay your debts on time and avoid late fees? Do you have some extra money that you can give when there are special needs that arise and good works that deserve support?

What important truth in *2 Corinthians 9:10-11* encourages a spirit of generosity when it comes to supporting good works and special needs that arise?

_____

_____

3. Are you able to give generously and regularly to the work of a local church? Is your giving to the Lord a high priority? Or, do you find yourself frequently saying, "I would love to give, but I just don't have any money left after I pay my bills?"

How were Christians in the first century church instructed to give? What guidelines in *1 Corinthians 16:1-2* would help you to develop healthy giving habits?

_____

_____

4. Are money needs and financial struggles creating problems that hinder you from spending time with people—family or otherwise—that you love and desire to serve?

The Philippian church gave frequently to help Paul in his Christian ministry. How are their gifts to him described in *Philippians 4:14-19*?

_____

_____

5. Does your schedule and budget allow adequate time and money to enjoy Christian fellowship with other believers in the form of home hospitality, special outings, retreats, and other such activities that are designed to nurture spiritual growth and maturity? (*3 John 5-8*)

What do you see in *Acts 2:42-47* that demonstrates the depth and quality of the love that these believers had for each other?

_____

_____

6. Are you pleased with your personal involvement in Christian disciplines such as prayer, Bible reading, active participation in a local church, and the like?

Read *Luke 10:38-42*. What can you learn and apply from these verses that would deepen you spiritually?

_____

_____

Analyzing Your Financial Personalities

Why is money such a sensitive subject for many couples to discuss? Why is it that our discussions frequently turn into debates? One possible explanation may be that you and your spouse have very different "financial personalities." You may be wired very differently.

For example, one spouse may have a money personality that promotes the idea, "Let's spend to acquire." However, the other mate is driven by the viewpoint, "We must save to retire." Big spenders can end up married to big savers. Or, one spouse may strongly prefer to avoid conversation about money matters. The other partner, however, may have an equally strong preference to talk about money and air things out thoroughly. It happens—avoiders end up married to worriers. Generous givers find themselves linked to stingy hoarders. Risk avoiders are married to risk takers. The super organized person can be partnered with someone who can never remember to keep receipts. Opposites do attract. It's no wonder that instead of connecting, we frequently collide.

Why are we wired so differently? How can we have such different approaches to money? In most cases, the biggest factor is what we learned during our growing up years. Some grew up in families where strict budget limits were set and honored. Money was tight and spending was controlled. Others were reared in homes where a budget was unheard of and where credit cards were used to bridge the gap between the end of the money and the end of the month. The joining of two individuals in marriage is the joining of two very different family cultures. It's easy to see how there can be a clash of money personalities. Couples should compare their views of money. Communicate! Listen to each other! Tell how money was handled in each of your families growing up and how you view money today as a result. Attempt to understand your mate's money personality. Remember that "different" does not necessarily mean "wrong."

Other factors that affect our financial personalities are such things as job history, emotional maturity, spiritual depth, and future goals. As marriage partners, we must be willing to compromise in the areas where we are different so that we can live together in Christian harmony.

Is It Time For A "Money-Checkup?"

Talking honestly and openly about money matters before and during marriage is essential to building a healthy and happy partnership. View your marriage as a business enterprise and keep it healthy and solvent—even profitable. It may be difficult to express your feelings and thoughts about money-related matters, yet it is imperative that marriage partners make time to communicate with each other and negotiate a money management plan that honors God and provides financial security for their family.

As you work through a money-checkup, you are likely to discover that each partner has a different definition of "wants" and "needs." There are likely to be differences of opinion. Decide on ground rules in advance of your "money-checkup" so that differences will not result in damages. Pray for wisdom. Stay calm. Listen to each other. Then, if things heat up, one person should take the dog for a walk. After a break, come back and try again. If you are in trouble financially and don't know what to do, get help immediately. Delay only causes the hole to get deeper. "Living happily ever after" depends on the willingness of each partner to be honest, responsible, and trustworthy in the way financial matters are managed.

A Checklist For A Money-Check-Up

1. **Determine your net worth.**
   - List your total income, including investments, checking and savings account amounts, money markets or CD's, employer benefits such as 401-K's, life insurance, real estate holdings, bonuses, inheritance, and so on. No one has all these kinds of income, but everyone has at least one.

2. **Decide on family goals.**
   - Too many aim for nothing and hit the bulls eye. It is so important to have definite financial plans for the future. Try to be realistic and agreeable about your goals. Remember it takes time to enjoy the benefits that others have worked for years to achieve.
   - You need to establish short-term goals. Are there preparations to make as you as you plan for the arrival of a child? Or, a short-term goal might be saving money to purchase furniture or to remodel a room in your house. Planning and discipline are not always easy, but they are crucial to good money management.
   - What are your long-term goals? Where would you like to be in five, ten, or twenty years from now? A five-year goal might be to put money aside each month for the down payment on a house. A twenty-year goal might be to set up a special fund for your children's education.
   - During your money-checkup, if you find that your goals are moving in opposite directions, you should identify these differences and find a workable plan to bridge these gaps as soon as possible.

3. **Carefully list your monthly expenses.**
   - Begin with the amount that you wish to give to the Lord's work—perhaps a local church or charity. Make this your number one priority. (*Luke 12:13-21*)

- What are your fixed expenses? This is money that we have promised to pay on specific dates and in specific amounts. Fixed expenses include things like rent or mortgage, utilities and installment debts, insurance premiums, property taxes, school tuition, an emergency fund, or health insurance. And don't forget that putting money into a savings or retirement plan is a fixed expense.

- What are your flexible expenses? These are expenses that vary from month to month. They include items such as food, clothing, gifts for all occasions, transportation, hobbies, personal care, and entertainment. Since these are not set amounts that are bound to contractual agreements, it may be that they can be cut back or cut out at times.

- Some of your expenses may be difficult to identify if you do not have receipts or good records. Estimate these items or keep track of them for a month or two before you complete this part of your budget.

4. **Establish a plan for spending—formulate a budget.**

   - Operating without a budget is like trying to steer a ship that has no rudder. Think of a budget as a plan to help you reach your goals. Knowing where you spend your money and where you can cut back is the first step toward effective money management.

   - Dave Ramsey says: "Just the act of putting together a budget is healthy for a marriage, apart from the financial benefits. Establishing a workable budget can help a hurting marriage simply because of the level of communication and cooperation required."

   - Resolve not to purchase items outside your budget unless you wait a set period of time. Avoid impulse buying.

   - Good budgets that are mutually agreed to and followed will decrease arguments, fees, secrets, calls from creditors, blood pressure, and impulsive spending.

   - Some are clueless as to how to formulate a budget. Get help if necessary. Find a trusted and competent friend who will assist.

   - Be realistic about family expenses remembering that emergencies and unexpected expenses will come up.

- Remember to be flexible since no plan is perfect. Practice patience and perseverance.
- Agree to have budget adjustment meetings. Your approach to budgeting must not lead you to become obsessive-compulsive about every nickel. Apply lots of common sense.

5. **Be full partners—resolve to have no financial secrets.**

- Most couples take a partnership approach in the management of their money. In most cases, it seems best to accept the reality that in marriage, assets and liabilities are no longer "yours" and "mine," but "ours."
- Ideally, there was a complete disclosure of assets and liabilities before marriage. No secrets or shocking discoveries. Every pertinent issue should be placed on the table. Information should not be withheld just because one spouse may not like what is revealed. Come clean!
- Since it is "our money," then "we" ought to agree on how the money will be spent. If one mate serves as the financial administrator, the other mate should serve as a full-time consultant. All records and accounts should be open and available to each partner. Each partner should be willing to hear and answer sincere money-related questions from the other partner without being defensive.
- No major purchases should be made unless both partners agree. The term "major purchase" should be clearly defined with a dollar value.
- It is wise, when possible, for each partner to have some "free money" to use as he or she sees fit.
- Be organized. Keep good records. Have a designated place for bills and receipts to be kept. Daily organization is required. Provide a safe place for important documents like leases, contracts, wills, titles, policies, and other such family documents. Resolve to be very careful in the way these documents are handled. Avoid carelessness.
- In many cases, it is wise for couples to utilize the services of a competent and certified financial planner who can provide wise counsel in money decisions. It is important for this person to understand Christian views and values.

The Danger Of Debt

The wicked borrow and do not repay, but the righteous give generously. (Psalm 37:21)

The borrower is servant to the lender. (Proverbs 22:7)

Do not be a man who strikes hands in pledge or puts up security for debts; if you lack the means to pay, your very bed will be snatched from under you. (Proverbs 22:26-27)

One financial advisor said, "Getting into debt is as easy as sliding down an icy embankment. Getting out of debt can be as difficult as climbing back up that same icy slope." The chief advantage of credit is convenience. The chief disadvantage of credit is convenience. People tend to do less planning and buy more when using credit. It seems to make it easier for us to redefine necessity. Be extremely cautious in the use of credit!

On every side, advertisers are saying, "Buy now. Pay later!" Too many buy now—and think later. No one tells us that if we buy now, we are likely to pay much more later. Credit is a privilege for which you must pay a price in most every case. Credit card companies are not foolish. They don't extend credit in order to lose money.

Why do we use credit? Because we want now what we cannot pay for now. In the purchase of a house, that may be a wise financial move. Rent must be paid anyway. If the house is carefully selected, it may appreciate in value over a period of time. Thus, if there are funds available for a down payment and we can afford the monthly payments, such a purchase might be wise. However, too many of us are using credit to purchase items that do not appreciate in value— food, fuel, clothes, and entertainment. We buy items before we can afford them. We pay the purchase price plus the interest charges for credit, while the purchased item itself continues to depreciate in value. Why? For the momentary pleasure that the item brings.

Protecting Your Credit Health

One big mistake that many couples make is neglecting their credit health. So quickly, families can accumulate numerous obligations including cell phone contracts, apartment rental agreements, car payments, and yes, those terrible credit card balances that can soon overwhelm their ability to pay. Some of these same individuals will have disagreements with their cell phone provider or apartment manager regarding service or payments and simply decide to teach them a lesson by not paying.

A failure to meet our legitimate obligations and pay our debts on time is sinful and damaging. Also, this behavior comes back to haunt us when we apply for additional credit to buy a car or purchase a house because these non-payments and late payments are reported to major credit monitoring agencies. These agencies provide payment information to lenders along with a score measuring your overall credit rating. These scores are widely used because they are fairly accurate in predicting credit worthiness.

A Debt-Free Lifestyle Is A Noble Goal

As much as possible, we should operate on the premise that to be able to afford an item means that you have the funds to pay for it. By postponing a purchase for a period of time, you can avoid those interest fees and the heavy burden of unpaid debt. Some couples learn and practice financial discipline by using a "cash only" approach to flexible household expenses. They create a system where cash is placed in envelopes marked "food," "hobbies," "entertainment," "gas," and "clothes." The general rule is when the money runs out, they're done until the next pay period. A quick look in an envelope answers the question whether or not money can be spent.

For people who are very disciplined and pay off outstanding balances at the end of each month, credit cards may be an option. In fact, the careful use of these cards can generate frequent flyer miles, cash rebates, or other perks. A good rule to follow if you use credit cards is to destroy the card the very first month you cannot pay off the balance.

Are You Are Caught In The Debt Trap?

If you are in financial bondage because of the misuse of credit, act decisively and quickly! Stop making charges! Destroy those cards! In many cases, it is wise to seek the help of a competent and trustworthy counselor who can help you to set up a plan for getting out of debt. The following conditions are clear indicators that serious money problems exist.

- You are unaware of how much you owe.
- You are spending money with the expectation that your income will increase in the future.
- You are taking cash advances on one credit card to pay off balances on other cards.
- You have more than two credit cards.

- You frequently pay only the minimum amount required rather than paying off the entire balance.
- You make monthly payments on your credit cards, yet fail to pay other bills.
- When you think about or begin being dishonest with money.

Escaping Financial Bondage Calls For A Change Of Heart

Good software and faster computers are helpful tools, but they will not correct problems of the heart. Before asking, "What are we spending for," maybe we need to ask, "Whom are we living for?" Pray for wisdom. (*James 1:5-6*) Recognize the need for self-control. (*Galatians 5:22*) Cultivate a spirit of contentment. (*Philippians 4:11-13; 1 Timothy 6:6-10*) Live at your address and avoid comparing your situation with others unless you compare it with those who have less. The key to financial freedom for Kingdom of God people is still found in those well-known words of Jesus.

> *Therefore I tell you, do not worry about your life, what you will eat or drink; or about your body, what you will wear. Is not life more important than food, and the body more important than clothes? Look at the birds of the air; they do not sow or reap or store away in barns, and yet your heavenly Father feeds them. Are you not much more valuable than they? Who of you by worrying can add a single hour to his life? And why do you worry about clothes? See how the lilies of the field grow. They do not labor or spin. Yet I tell you that not even Solomon in all his splendor was dressed like one of these. If that is how God clothes the grass of the field, which is here today and tomorrow is thrown into the fire, will he not much more clothe you, O you of little faith? So do not worry, saying, 'What shall we eat?' or 'What shall we drink?' or 'What shall we wear?' For the pagans run after all these things, and your heavenly Father knows that you need them. But seek first his kingdom and his righteousness, and all these things will be given to you as well. Therefore do not worry about tomorrow, for tomorrow will worry about itself. Each day has enough trouble of its own. (Matthew 6:25-33)*

Harmony Building Exercises

1. The spirit of consumerism is strong. Every time we turn on the TV, listen to the radio, read the newspaper or magazines, or go into stores we are

being influenced to buy. We must develop smart shopping habits and a strong defense against the worldly traps set by Satan to take away that which God has given us. Make a list of smart shopping habits that will help us to be good stewards of all that God has given us.

2. Debt can be damaging. Excessive debt can be a major hindrance when it comes to honoring biblical commands and principles. Can you identify three specific commands given in the New Testament that excessive debt may hinder a Christian from obeying?

3. The message from today's culture is that material things do provide ultimate happiness. Is this true? Explain your answer.

4. Having too little of this world's goods can be a difficult experience and this is why there are many passages in the Scriptures that pertain to compassion for the poor. Yet, there are also many passages in the Bible that warn us of the dangers of wealth. Using the book of *Proverbs*, identify five passages that describe the dangers of wealth.

5. Identify an experienced Christian couple that has achieved a high level of marital harmony when it comes to money management. Ask this couple to share their wisdom and some of the secrets they have learned over the years. (*Titus 2:1-5*)

CHAPTER 7
Harmony In Marital Romance

Holy Romance—Not Hollywood Romance

In high definition, living color, and surround sound, Hollywood bombards us with the message that exciting and exhilarating romance is experienced in steamy affairs and secretive rendezvous with a partner other than your marriage mate. The frequent message of the popular media is, "If an extra-marital encounter will feel good and make you happy, go for it. You only live once. Just do it."

This is a sick distortion of true love and an ugly perversion of the Creator's beautiful plan. God teaches us that the happiest, healthiest, and holiest love relationship is with one loyal marriage partner to whom you are deeply committed for a lifetime. God's approach to love and romance unites two lives in a pledge of marital fidelity before two bodies are joined in a union of sexual pleasure. First comes the pledge—and then the pleasure.

Hollywood's version of romance displays and promotes a cheap counterfeit of the high and holy love to which God calls us in a monogamous marriage relationship. The reader should make a clear distinction between the two approaches as the material in this chapter is studied.

A Reality Check On Romance

Beware! Don't allow fantasy to intrude on reality.

If you take your cue from popular movies, magazines, and songs, you could embrace the mistaken view that romance in marriage means that every day is to be filled with breathless passion and continual pleasure. Not so! Don't be misled. Such a view can cause one partner to perceive that he or she is being cheated and make unrealistic demands that are not sustainable or realistic. The patterns of romance for each couple are different and one size does not fit all. You must know and learn to live compatibly with your partner.

The truth is that a strong marriage can not and should not be built on romantic feelings. The solid base of a stable marriage is commitment to God and each other. On this foundation, there will be a strong sense of mutual respect, trust, and caring. It is these qualities that continually prompt us to be nurturing toward the other person in spite of inadequacies or differences that may exist. Patience, compromise, understanding, and acceptance of one another are the qualities that keep the pipes of love and romance unclogged and flowing. In every healthy marriage, there is a natural ebb and flow—mountaintops and valleys, some days of living color and other days that show up as black and white. There should be no periods of total blackout. The important thing to understand is that intense romantic chemistry is not constant—this is an unrealistic expectation! Beware!

Marriage Is For Lovers

In the beginning, God looked over His creative handiwork. Only one part of the finished product did He consider not good—Adam living in isolation without suitable companionship. Seeing this need, God took action.

> God saw all that he had made, and it was very good. And there was evening, and there was morning—the sixth day. (Genesis 1:31)

> The LORD God said, "It is not good for the man to be alone. I will make a helper suitable for him." (Genesis 2:18)

> So the LORD God caused the man to fall into a deep sleep; and while he was sleeping, he took one of the man's ribs and closed up the place with flesh. Then the LORD God made a woman from the rib He had taken out of the man, and he brought her to the man. The man said, "This is now bone of my bones and flesh of my flesh; she shall be called 'woman,' for she was taken out of man." For this reason a man will leave his father and mother and be united to his wife, and they will become one flesh. The man and his wife were both naked, and they felt no shame. (Genesis 2:21-25)

In his commentary on Genesis, Hebrew scholar Dr. John Willis says of the above passage, "These words exhibit man's excitement and inexpressible joy over finding a companion that suited him perfectly." (Genesis, John T. Willis, Sweet Publishing Co., Austin, Texas, 1979). When a lonely Adam looked at a lovely Eve, he must have

yelled, "WOW!" Adam and Eve were created by God to be full partners in marriage. Each needed the other to be complete. They were
to enjoy spiritual, emotional, and sexual intimacy—the essence of
true romance. The physiological and psychological designs of males
and females make it obvious that we were crafted by God to be
joined together as one flesh in a fully shared life. It is crucial that
we not lose the "WOW-effect" in our marriages! Yes, in God's design,
marriage is definitely for lovers!

But What Happens To "The Wow?"

For far too many married couples, the sizzle quickly turns into a
fizzle. Is there something in the small print of a marriage license
that reads, "Once you are married, it is expected that tenderness,
courtesy, passion, and romance will cease?" What is it about being
married that seems to result in a loss of romantic energy and creativity? Someone said, "If love is a dream, marriage is the alarm clock."
Another cynic said, "The period of engagement is like an exciting
introduction to a dull book." Sadly, in the daily grind of married life,
romance is often the first thing to go.

Without warmth, tenderness, and intimacy, marriage can be like
eating shredded wheat with no milk, sugar, or strawberries. Do you
recall those wonderful days of romance when you were seriously
courting your spouse—the sheer pleasure of being together, the an-
ticipation, the excitement, the planning, the wooing, the courtesy,
and the exhilaration? You could not look at each other without smil-
ing. But, what happens to former lovers? Why do the fires wane and
the sparks of romance go out?

Common Hindrances To Marital Romance

Couples must work at maintaining a healthy kind of romantic
interaction with each other. What are some conditions that can make
this a difficult challenge?

1. The everydayness of human life.

The wear and tear of daily life can take its toll on romance—
illnesses, bills, job stressors, addictions, conflict, pregnancies, pro-
motions, demotions, or any other experience, good or bad, that puts
physical, emotional, or spiritual distance between you and your
mate. There are days when any human being is going to feel that
his or her birthstone is the "grindstone."

2. Poor role models from the formative years.

Some people never saw affection and warmth in the growing up years of life and it feels foreign to them. Many people tend to live out what they saw modeled by their parents or other significant adults. If you saw marriage partners who were distant, detached, cold, or violent, be careful that you don't replay those mental tapes in your own thinking and practice them in your marriage.

3. Embracing cultural stereotypes.

Some people buy into the stereotype that if you are married, you don't express love or practice romance. This myth has been perpetuated over the years. If asked why there is no excitement or romance in their relationship, some couples would simply answer, "Because we are married!" Beware of peer pressure. Beware of "the boys" or "the girls." They don't have good marriages and they don't want you to have one.

4. Moral failure and sin that damages the union.

The fabric of marriage is ripped and torn when the vows of faithfulness and fidelity are broken. One night stands, prolonged affairs, or addiction to pornography can result in great physical, emotional, and spiritual damage. In some cases, the wounds are so deep that healing does not occur.

5. Unresolved conflict and lingering bitterness.

When the emotional and relational pipes are clogged, nothing flows. Marital closeness and intimacy cannot thrive where there are issues and controversies that keep spilling bitterness into the relationship.

6. A negative emotional climate that fills the home.

When a home has too much negativity, sarcasm, criticism, and argumentation, the romantic temperature drops significantly. Romance and genuine marital sensitivity can only survive in a climate of emotional warmth.

7. Inattention to physical appearance and hygiene.

For some people, getting comfortable in a marriage relationship becomes permission to grow careless about personal upkeep and hygiene. Melissa Hamilton refers to this practice as "sliding into sloppy." It is important to never quit trying to be appealing to your mate. The factors that were important in wooing and winning your partner continue to be important in keeping him or her.

8. Marriages that are too child-centered.

Children bring great joy and fulfillment into our lives and they deserve our tender love and careful attention. However, with the arrival of children, some couples seem to lose the ability to keep healthy romance and intimacy alive in their relationships. Couples mistakenly conclude that the children cannot take care of themselves, but the marriage can. One or both partners can lose their sense of identity as a lover and begin to exist solely as mom or dad. Excessive child-centeredness can sometimes be a mask for deep-seated problems in a marriage.

It is very important to find and maintain a balance between "couple needs" and "children's needs." In fact, enjoying closeness and intimacy as a couple is an essential part of being good parents. One of the greatest gifts we give our kids is the model of a mom and dad who truly love each other.

Thus, making time for each other as a couple is essential. Attending PTO meetings, funerals, and weddings together can never be legitimate substitutes for couple-time. And, when there are those special occasions to enjoy time together, make sure not to sabotage the experience by feeling guilty or sad. It is important to remember that, in one sense, the husband-wife relationship is the primary relationship in the family. When the kids are grown and have established their own homes, you as marriage partners will still be together and, hopefully, have additional years to enjoy. Make sure that even though your nest is empty of children, it remains full of affection and tender love for each other. Keep doing your "homework" so that the person who sits across the table from you continues to be your friend and lover rather than a stranger.

Rekindling The Spark In Marriage

How do you get the romantic spark back if it's gone? Or, how do you fan the fire that is now flickering? First, you must decide to take action and pray for wisdom from God as you plan your strategy.

Perhaps we need to learn a valuable lesson from the principle taught in *Revelation 2:4-5*. The Lord commanded a lukewarm church to remember the importance of practicing *"first love."* Specifically, the Lord said to these believers who had lost their spiritual fire, *"Do the things you did at first."* One possible way to rekindle the fires of romance is to "do the things we did at first!" While we cannot go back in time and fully relive our courtship experiences, we can practice a style of relating that resembles that way it was at first. There can be a restoration of genuine warmth, caring, closeness, and intimacy.

Often, it is the "little things" that are actually "big things" when it comes to nurturing each other. Each couple must find their everyday way of relating and romancing. We never get too old to show tenderness and sensitivity to a partner. Work at being the kind of person that your mate will desire to be with. Do all that you can to improve the quality and quantity of daily communication. Here are some ideas that may be helpful.

1. If what you are doing is not working, do something different.

A marital groove can eventually feel like a grave. This must not continue. What can you do differently? As you consider alternatives, both partners must be aware and agreeable. Give up what is not working and resolve to practice a different way of expressing love and demonstrating consideration for each other.

The change does not have to involve something that is expensive or exotic. A trip to Paris is not necessary. It may have to be a friendly visit to your local Dairy Queen or a nice walk where the two of you can hold hands and share your feelings with and for each other. Make the time. Plan the event—whatever it is. When possible, it is good for couples to save some extra money for a one or two night get-away—including a competent caretaker for the children. Make these couple-times good and memorable times. Let them refresh you as individuals and as a couple. Everyone wins when this happens!

2. Keep an open and positive attitude toward your mate.

Re-kindling the spark of healthy romance is so much easier to achieve when both partners are truly partners in the endeavor. The positive actions on the part of one mate can certainly make a difference, but when both are actively involved in the process, greater and faster results can occur.

If your partner reaches out to you, reach back. If overtures are made to re-connect romantically, give positive feedback. Consider the possibility of being the one who initiates the process. When your spouse invites you to be involved in an appropriate activity that will close physical and emotional gaps in the relationship, be cheerfully responsive. Be careful not to pour cold water on a rekindled spark of romance. If problems exist, communicate. If problems persist, get help.

3. Resolve to make intimacy your way of life.

While it is true that every day cannot be Valentine's Day, make sure that love and romance occur at times other than Valentine's Day. Find ways every day to maintain closeness in your relationship—an affirmation of love, a touch, a note, a card, a phone call, a surprise gift, a listening ear, a walk, a talk, or a favor. These are the small things that send the clear message, "You are and will always be the most important person in my life!" Be willing to make daily deposits of love, communication, and affirmation as you live and love in marriage. This is real romance.

4. Cultivate a close relationship with God.

Walking in intimacy with God makes you a better lover and marriage partner. God is love. As we walk with Him, we learn the essence of true love. As His spirit lives in us, we learn to give, forgive, and forbear.

Don't Get Discouraged! Don't Quit Trying!

Marital muscles must be built just as physical muscles are built. It takes hard work, patience, and time. When you fail and fall, don't quit. Get up and try again. Keep praying and asking God to help you as a couple.

If the spark of romance is present in your marriage, fan it!

If the spark is flickering and fading, act quickly to revive it!

If the spark is gone, do whatever it takes to resurrect it!

Harmony Building Exercises

1. Discuss some of the ways that Hollywood's version of romance can adversely affect the way we look at our marriage partners and view marital romance.

2. Many people in today's culture are living together without marriage. Besides the fact that these relationships are sinful and adulterous, what other relational negatives can you see in these living arrangements?

3. If males and females were asked to define and describe romance, what noticeable differences do you think might surface?

4. Read *1 Corinthians 6:12-20*. What principles of truth are taught in this passage that help us to understand how exceedingly sinful it is to experience a sexual union outside of marriage?

5. What spoke to your heart in this chapter regarding the importance of loving and nurturing our children, yet not building our lives around them? Share your thoughts and ideas.

6. Why can it be difficult to rekindle the sparks of romance once the fire has waned?

7. Identify an older Christian couple whose nest is empty of children but still full of love and romance. Have this couple share some of their "marital secrets" as to how they have continued to preserve intimacy and practice romance over so many years. (*Titus 2:1-5*)

8. Discuss the idea that intimacy with God makes you a better lover and marriage partner. If you believe this is a valid idea, share your reasons why.

CHAPTER 8

Sexual Harmony In Marriage

Our Desire For Sexual Expression—Is It Of God?

Who created the male and female anatomy?

God did!

Who designed the male and female bodies so that they respond to sexual stimulation and enable us to enjoy immense pleasure as husbands and wives?

God did!

Who brought the first male and female together in marriage and encouraged them to *"become one flesh"*?

God did!

Sexual pleasure in marriage was God's idea. After creating our bodies and equipping us to function sexually, His assessment was, *This is "very good."* (*Genesis 1:31*) What kind of God would fashion the two bodies as He did, place within each a desire for the other, and then look with disfavor when two marriage partners experience and fully enjoy their sexual union? Realism calls for us to acknowledge the strong desire created in man and woman for a sexual union. This is by God's design. In fact, the first commandment that God gave to Adam and Eve was, *"Be fruitful and increase in number."* (*Genesis 1:28*)

The sexual relationship is a marvelous gift that God designed for marriage partners. When approached in this way, it can and should be enjoyed to the fullest and viewed as a God-honoring way to express human love.

God's Plan For Sexual Expression Is Under Attack

Jesus referred to the society in which He lived as an *"adulterous and sinful generation."* (*Mark 8:38*) What words do you think He might use to describe ours?

While waiting in an airport, this writer overheard a conversation by two young women who were seated inches away just to his backside. With laughter, one of the females said to her companion, "I met my boyfriend three years ago and everything about the formation of our relationship has occurred in reverse order. First, we decided that we would live together. Then, we had a child together. This summer we took a seven-day cruise together for our honeymoon. And, now this fall, we are planning to get married." These ladies laughed heartily. God's heart grieved.

Sadly, this airport conversation describes the view and practice of too many in today's culture. It reflects a total ignorance of or disregard for the plan that God has for men and women to express and enjoy their sexuality as committed marriage partners. Our culture is in the midst of a terrible storm—it's raining hard on our "cultural house." The waters are rising all around us and there is clear evidence that the foundation underneath is eroding and crumbling. We are reaping the consequences of a widespread departure from biblical standards and Christian guidelines. Judeo-Christian values are not just being questioned—they are being disputed, denied, and despised!

The Christian Home And Church Must Speak Up

Honoring what is revealed in the Word of God must always have priority over being relevant in the secular world. There is a need for us to blow the dust off our Bibles and carefully restudy the biblical truths related to human sexuality and marriage. These binding principles must be taught in our churches and lived out in our families. Our views and values are not to be shaped by the distorted and sinful messages being promoted by Hollywood and the secular media. The Bible does speak clearly on the subject of human sexuality and so should we.

Joe Beam, President of Family Dynamics, in Nashville, Tennessee, writes:

> It appears that many parents and churches have avoided the subject of sex. The thinking often goes like this, "If we talk about sex, our teens and singles will want to do it. To keep from exciting those urges, we won't discuss anything to do with sex. So we'll just tell them, 'Don't do it!' and leave it at that. They'll figure out the good parts when they marry."

> Of course, that "silent approach" fails in several ways. First, not talking about sex to people who are discovering their own sexual-

ity is to leave them to be shaped by the world. We've seen the consequences of that! Second, avoiding sexual conversations doesn't decrease curiosity or desire. Just the opposite—it makes temptation stronger. Finally, leaving couples unprepared for love life in marriage often creates all sorts of marital distress in the future. It's the truth that sets us free, not ignorance.

The Bible Teaches That Sexual Pleasure Is To Be Enjoyed By One Man And One Woman

In this age of "sexploitation," a growing number of people are questioning the biblical truth that marriage is for one man and one woman. There are even some in the religious community who are denying this age-old principle. What does the Bible say?

Then God said, "Let us make man in our image, in our likeness, and let them rule over the fish of the sea and the birds of the air, over the livestock, over all the earth, and over all the creatures that move along the ground." So God created man in his own image, in the image of God he created him; male and female he created them. God blessed them and said to them, "Be fruitful and increase in number; fill the earth and subdue it." (Genesis 1:26-28)

The picture in Genesis is that God created *"males and females"* to be counterparts—with the two differing entities coming together to be one. The biblical record continues:

The LORD God said, "It is not good for the man to be alone. I will make a helper suitable for him." Now the LORD God had formed out of the ground all the beasts of the field and all the birds of the air. He brought them to the man to see what he would name them; and whatever the man called each living creature, that was its name. So the man gave names to all the livestock, the birds of the air and all the beasts of the field. But for Adam no suitable helper was found. So the LORD God caused the man to fall into a deep sleep; and while he was sleeping, he took one of the man's ribs and closed up the place with flesh. Then the LORD God made a woman from the rib he had taken out of the man, and he brought her to the man. The man said, "This is now bone of my bones and flesh of my flesh; she shall be called 'woman,' for she was taken out of man." For this reason a man will leave his father and mother and be united to his wife, and they will become one flesh. The man and his wife were both naked, and they felt no shame. (*Genesis 2:18-25*)

God recognized that Adam—a male—needed a counterpart for companionship, intimacy, and sexual fulfillment. Thus, God created Eve—a female. The woman that God created to be a *"suitable partner"* did not look like, think like, feel like, walk like, sound like, function like, act like, or even smell like...Adam! Could God have created another...Adam? He could have, but He didn't.

When it was time to design a partner with whom Adam could enjoy companionship, intimacy, and sexuality, God made a female—not another male. Two naked Adams could never experience the beautiful reality of *"becoming one flesh"* as was the case with Adam and Eve. When you try to create a unity of two bodies that were not designed for unity, you make ugly and sinful what God designed to be beautiful and holy!

In *Genesis 1:1-25*, we have the biblical record of everything that was created with the exception of humans. And, here's what is interesting. In the description of all God's creative activity over the first five days, gender—that is, maleness and femaleness—is not mentioned even one time in those verses. All the animals that God made were created male and female, but there's no mention of that fact—no emphasis at all on gender. It was not something to which God called attention in His Word.

Yet, on day six, when God created human beings, the inspired account says:

> *"So God created man in his own image, in the image of God he created him; MALE AND FEMALE HE CREATED THEM."* (*Genesis 1:27*). Emphasis added.

It was only in connection with humans that gender was mentioned. God carefully designed the male and female so that they could enjoy intimacy and experience sexual oneness. The Creator's plan for marriage and family is clearly revealed in Scripture and to deviate from that model is to invite physical, emotional, social, and spiritual disaster.

When Jesus was teaching on marriage, where did He go for a model? He went all the way back to the *Genesis* record because He knew that this was God's universal model for human intimacy and sexuality. (*Matthew 19:7-9*) The "Genesis-model" had one man joined to one woman in the relationship of marriage.

The Bible Teaches That Sexual Pleasure Is To Be Enjoyed Only In Marriage

According to God's plan, sexual intercourse is to be enjoyed only by committed marriage partners. The "body language" that is expressed in this physical union shouts a message of "oneness." Sexual intimacy was designed by God as a way of demonstrating a deep and permanent commitment to another person. Sexual unity is a non-verbal way of saying, "We are one! We are committed! We will remain together!" Bodily actions have meanings as much as words do. Until there is a "life union" between two people, there should no "body union." What does the Bible say?

> *Marriage should be honored by all, and the marriage bed kept pure, for God will judge the adulterer and all the sexually immoral. (Hebrews 13:4)*

This is a very interesting verse. The Greek word for *"bed"* is *"koite,"* (koy-tay) which is the term for "sexual intercourse." Within the context of marriage, sexual intercourse is pure and honorable. Outside marriage, the act becomes impure and dishonorable.

In *1 Corinthians 7*, Paul makes it clear that marriage is the God-designed and God-sanctioned way to prevent sexual immorality. He writes:

> *Now for the matters you wrote about: It is good for a man not to marry. But since there is so much immorality, each man should have his own wife, and each woman her own husband. The husband should fulfill his marital duty to his wife, and likewise the wife to her husband. The wife's body does not belong to her alone but also to her husband. In the same way, the husband's body does not belong to him alone but also to his wife. Do not deprive each other except by mutual consent and for a time, so that you may devote yourselves to prayer. Then come together again so that Satan will not tempt you because of your lack of self-control. I say this as a concession, not as a command. I wish that all men were as I am. But each man has his own gift from God; one has this gift, another has that. (1 Corinthians 7:1-7)*

This passage must be understood against the backdrop of historical circumstances in ancient Corinth. In this city were numerous extremists who were at opposite poles regarding the matter of human sexuality. Some advocated free sex, while others advocated no sex. The latter group seems to have embraced the idea that there was a "higher spirituality" in celibacy and even encouraged married people to abstain from the practice of sex.

In the first verse of *1 Corinthians 7*, Paul writes, *"...it is good for a man not to marry."* Paul is repeating what some misguided Corinthians were saying. This statement is not expressive of Paul's general and overall view of marriage. Not at all! In the chapter, he does mention some benefits to remaining single, yet his comments must be understood in light of the fact that some are endowed with a special gift from God that enables them to live celibately whereas others are not so endowed. (*1 Corinthians 7:7*) Also, it should be pointed out that extenuating circumstances which existed at the time Paul was writing had great bearing upon his comments regarding the desirability of remaining single. (*1 Corinthians 7:25-35*)

The strong and clear message of this passage in *1 Corinthians 7* is that marriage between a husband and wife is the only God-approved way to prevent sexual immorality. Read it again. *"But since there is so much immorality, each man should have his own wife, and each woman her own husband."* (verse 2)

The Bible Teaches That Sexual Pleasure Is To Be Experienced In Marriage

The holy God endorses sexual pleasure in marriage. He does not turn away when a husband and wife enjoy their sexual union. This is clear in the Scriptures.

> *Drink water from your own well—share your love only with your wife. Why spill the water of your springs in the streets, having sex with just anyone? You should reserve it for yourselves. Never share it with strangers. Let your wife be a fountain of blessing for you. Rejoice in the wife of your youth. She is a loving deer, a graceful doe. Let her breasts satisfy you always. May you always be captivated by her love.* (*Proverbs 5:15-19 NLT*)

God included one entire book in the Bible—*The Song of Songs*—to describe the romantic love and sexual interaction between a husband and wife. It is a song that praises the love that exists between marriage mates. (*Song of Songs 3:11; 5:1*) The following verses from this Old Testament document illustrate the sexual delight that God wants husbands and wives to experience:

This is Solomon's song of songs, more wonderful than any other. Young Woman: Kiss me and kiss me again, for your love is sweeter than wine. My lover is like a sachet of myrrh lying between my breasts. (*Song of Songs 1:1-2, 13 NLT*)

I said, "I will climb the palm tree and take hold of its fruit." May your breasts be like grape clusters, and the fragrance of your breath like apples. May your kisses be as exciting as the best wine, flowing gently over lips and teeth."

Young Woman: "I am my lover's, and he claims me as his own." (*Song of Songs 7:8-10 NLT*)

For some, it may take time to become comfortable with the idea that we can experience sexual pleasure. There is no reason for an emotional or spiritual disconnect between a sanctified life in Jesus and a sexually fulfilling experience with your marriage partner. When biblical principles are honored, there can be a wonderful harmony between spiritual fullness and sexual fulfillment.

The Bible Warns Against Sexual Adultery

Faithfulness is the cornerstone of marriage. Adultery, plain and simple, is sexual intercourse with a person who is not your husband or wife. Adultery is wrong—always wrong. The commandments of God are not only right, they are best for us. Living and loving in the will of God is the course of wisdom.

For wisdom will enter your heart, and knowledge will be pleasant to your soul. Discretion will protect you, and understanding will guard you. Wisdom will save you from the ways of wicked men, from men whose words are perverse, who leave the straight paths to walk in dark ways, who delight in doing wrong and rejoice in the perverseness of evil, whose paths are crooked and who are devious in their ways. It will save you also from the adulteress, from the wayward wife with her seductive words, who has left the partner of her youth and ignored the covenant she made before God. For her house leads down to death and her paths to the spirits of the dead. None who go to her return or attain the paths of life. (*Proverbs 2:10-19*)

Why be captivated, my son, by an adulteress? Why embrace the bosom of another man's wife? For a man's ways are in full view of the LORD, and he examines all his paths. The evil deeds of a wicked man ensnare him; the cords of his sin hold him fast. He will die for lack of discipline, led astray by his own great folly. (Proverbs 5:20-23)

This is the way of an adulteress: She eats and wipes her mouth and says, "I've done nothing wrong." (Proverbs 30:20)

Jesus shocked the people of His day by redefining the Law of Moses. He not only condemned the act of adultery, but the lust that motivates it. Moses said, "Don't do it." Jesus said, "Don't even think about doing it."

"You have heard that it was said, 'Do not commit adultery.' But I tell you that anyone who looks at a woman lustfully has already committed adultery with her in his heart." (Matthew 5:27-28)

In teaching us how to combat sexual lust, Jesus spoke in very graphic metaphorical terms. We are to take His words seriously, but not literally. The source of the sin is in the heart—not the limbs of the body.

If your right eye causes you to sin, gouge it out and throw it away. It is better for you to lose one part of your body than for your whole body to be thrown into hell. And if your right hand causes you to sin, cut it off and throw it away. It is better for you to lose one part of your body than for your whole body to go into hell. (Matthew 5:29-30)

Beware Of Today's Moral Climate—It Can Be Infectious

For centuries, humans have bought into the lie that a secretive, adulterous affair with someone other than your marriage partner is more exciting than love in marriage. This message is supported today by much of what we see, hear, and read. There was a time when sexual monogamy was encouraged and rewarded by societal institutions and conditions. Families stressed the importance of character, communities rewarded high moral standards, employers encouraged marital fidelity, and the religious community stressed the necessity of biblical guidelines—even the government allowed the presence and practice of Judeo-Christian principles. These were foundational blocks that helped to provide steadiness and stability. Things have changed!

Many of these foundational blocks that supported marital fidelity now have major cracks or have fallen apart altogether. In our secular culture, even Christians can be adversely affected by the moral climate of the world around them. Peter warns believers, *"Be self-controlled and alert. Your enemy the devil prowls around like a roaring lion looking for someone to devour."* (*1 Peter 5:8*) To Christians who lived in the capital city of the godless Roman Empire, Paul said, *"Don't copy the behavior and customs of this world, but let God transform you into a new person by changing the way you think. Then you will learn to know God's will for you, which is good and pleasing and perfect."* (*Romans 12:2 NLT*)

Avoiding Sexual Temptation In The Daily Workplace

Studies show that a high percentage of people who have extramarital affairs meet their unlawful partners at work. In view of this threat, the course of wisdom calls for us to be extremely cautious in the following areas:

1. Avoid private lunches and coffee breaks with co-workers of the opposite sex.
2. Be especially careful when forced to engage in business travel where males and females are together.
3. Avoid private business sessions—as much as possible, meet in groups.
4. Avoid excessive and inappropriate physical touching.
5. Avoid frequent conversations about your personal life and family or marriage problems.
6. Speak openly about your spouse and family. Display pictures of your loved ones in conspicuous places.

Avoiding The Temptation To Misuse The Internet And Media

The World Wide Web can become a snare that entangles us and leads to moral failure and sin. We must use caution as we enter the world of cyberspace. The Internet can become an "electronic lover" that steals time and attention from your spouse. Carefully consider how you can avoid the following traps that Satan will place in your path.

1. Chat rooms can be a tremendous danger to a marriage—avoid sites designed for meeting people and socializing.

2. Keep computers in open spaces where secrets cannot be kept.

3. Limit your time on-line.

4. Avoid pornography—it is addictive.

5. Be careful what music you listen to, what movies and TV you watch, and generally avoid any stimulus that provokes unhealthy and ungodly thoughts and desires.

6. Remember that infidelity does not always include sexual intercourse.

7. Emotional infidelity can breach marital trust and become as debilitating and damaging to your marriage as actual adultery.

The God Who Forgives And Allows Us To Start Over

God wants His children to practice sexual purity, but the age-old reality is that some of us make bad decisions and commit immoral acts. Adultery is a sin, but it is not the unpardonable sin.

King David is referred to as *"a man after [God's] own heart,"* (*Acts 13:22*), yet in a moment of weakness and sin, he lusted after a beautiful woman and committed the sin of adultery with her. (*2 Samuel 11*) However, David's walk with God did not end with this moral fall. Because of his penitent spirit, God forgave David. (*Psalm 32, 51*) There are other examples to illustrate the point. The Samaritan woman (*John 4*) and the woman who was caught in the act of adultery (*John 8*) broke the law and heart of God by their immorality, yet they were forgiven. No matter what you have done and no matter how guilty you feel, you can be forgiven and restored to fellowship and friendship with God. Through genuine repentance and confession, you can hear Jesus say:

Neither do I condemn you. . .Go now and leave your life of sin." (John 8:11)

Harmony Building Exercises

1. Since we see and hear so much in our culture about sex, is it wise and practical for the church to expand this conversation by teaching biblical principles related to sexuality? Explain your response.

2. Do you agree or disagree with the quote by Joe Beam that appears in this chapter? Which is the greater risk—teaching what the Bible says about sexuality or not teaching these truths?

3. Read *Genesis 39:1-20*. What practical lessons can we learn and apply from this incident that will strengthen us as married couples and as individuals?

4. Read *2 Samuel 11:1-27*. What practical lessons can we learn and apply from this incident that will strengthen us as married couples and as individuals?

5. One husband who was sexually unfaithful to his wife said, "My immorality was not the result of one big step on one particular day, but a series of small steps over a longer period of time." If you were speculating, what "small steps" do you think he might have taken?

6. What practical suggestions and guidelines could you offer to married people who live in the daily workplace as to how they can avoid sexual temptation and immorality?

7. What more can local churches do to promote marital fidelity and prevent marital infidelity among believers? How can we make a difference in the culture-at-large?

8. Post-moderns are suspicious of those who make "universal truth claims." For example, they would view the binding of biblical principles as an effort to marginalize and oppress the rights of others. They refuse to allow any single defining source for truth and reality, and stress the importance of diversity, plurality, and tolerance. How should this reality in our culture affect our efforts to teach the Bible and uphold moral absolutes?

9. From your vantage point, would you say that postmodern concerns for plurality, diversity, and tolerance have led to a more stable and secure society? Explain.

10. What are some practical steps that we can take in our Christian homes to adequately prepare our children for a positive, healthy, and wholesome approach to sexuality in their marriages?

CHAPTER 9

Harmony With The In-Laws

Getting Serious About In-Laws

Many counselors tell us that the three biggest problems in marriage are money, sex, and in-laws. In this chapter, we focus on the latter topic.

When it comes to in-law relationships, we have mostly told jokes rather than engaging in helpful study and constructive conversations that promote healthy and happy relationships within our extended families. This is an area of married life that can be extremely tough for some couples. Most families have had at least a slight taste of in-law disharmony and know firsthand how troublesome this can be.

At many weddings, you will hear a parent say, "I'm not losing a son or daughter. I'm gaining an additional son or daughter." It's such a nice thing to say and in ideal cases, it works out this way. However, this can have hidden snags because the person you gain through marriage is an adult who has been shaped and influenced by another family orientation. The differences that a son-in-law or daughter-in-law bring into the original family circle can result in controversies or conflicts, which can be divisive.

Typically There Is A Hostile Triangle

Frequently, when there are in-law problems affecting a marriage, you will discover a "hostile triangle" with one person caught in the middle of two feuding parties. Each triangle is different—you must fill in the blanks if the problem exists in your marriage. Frequently, the "hostile triangle" involves one individual caught between a marriage partner and one or more members of his or her family. The person caught in this emotional vise may be feeling tremendous pressure to accommodate members of his or her family of origin, while at the same time trying to appease a spouse who is feeling irritated or angry toward the in-laws. If this vicious triangle continues, it can eventually lead to years of family tension, hostility, alienation, or even divorce.

Myths, Stereotypes, And False Notions About In-Laws

For years, we have heard the in-law jokes and stories, most of which have been negative and degrading. Such negative conditioning within our culture has caused some to begin their marriages with unfair and inaccurate assumptions regarding in-law relationships. Some of these myths, stereotypes, and false notions are:

1. In-laws are unimportant and insignificant in a marriage relationship.

This is false! Relationships within the extended family are vital and important to any marriage. The relatives of your mate will be a part of your world for the rest of your life. Value these individuals as people who are precious and important to your marriage partner and who must be valuable to you as well.

Peaceful and loving co-existence with in-laws can be a great blessing and important stabilizing force in your home. It can help to maintain a sweet unity between you and your mate and keep you from winding up in opposite corners. Do all that you can to make sure the relatives of your partner are viewed and valued as "IN"-laws and not "OUT"-laws.

2. I am only marrying one person—not the entire family.

This is faulty thinking. While it's true that your marriage license contains the names of only two people who are entering into the partnership of marriage, the fact is that the person you marry has strong and binding ties to a larger family circle that is likely to always be a significant presence and power in his or her life. If you attempt to cut off the family of your mate, you are likely to pay a huge toll in family harmony and marital unity. When you marry "your partner," you are marrying into "the partnership" that he or she has had with a family of origin for many years.

3. Solving problems with my mate's people will be a lot easier after we are married.

This is fantasy thinking. If there are skirmishes before marriage, there is likely to be warfare afterward. Saying, "I do" in a wedding ceremony does not cause the problems to suddenly go away. In fact, the bad feelings that surfaced before marriage could get even worse after marriage.

4. The view that my marriage partner had of his or her family before we married will never change.

Time has a way of changing how we view people and problems in our lives—especially family members. During the years of adolescence and early adulthood, it is fairly predictable that there will be conflict between parents and children. This is normal.

However, as we mature, leave home, and live separately from our parents, we discover the pleasant reality that old wounds tend to heal and broken relationships with parents get mended. Parents, who may have been viewed as the enemy when we were single, will in many cases become our adult friends when we are married. As this process unfolds, you may discover that a partner who saw things "your way" before marriage may begin to see things "the in-law's way" after marriage.

5. We will move away from the in-laws so that they cannot affect or interfere with our lives.

Have you forgotten that we live in a world of airplanes, interstate highways, e-mail, telephones, video cams, and instant messaging? You can run, but you cannot hide. In this world of amazing mobility, you cannot move away from people. In fact, the greater the distance, the more the sparks of emotional attachment may be fanned. Plus, you may find that you can't escape "the family" of a mate since "family values and traits" may have been deeply ingrained in your marriage partner. Don't forget the old saying, "You can take the boy or girl out of the country, but you can't take the country out of the boy or girl."

6. In-laws are the enemy—always bothersome and difficult.

Some are conditioned to assume that all in-laws want to control and interfere. This is not true. Beware of prejudice, which can result in premature condemnation. In-laws should be considered innocent until proven guilty. And, even when mistakes have been made, the Lord Jesus can help us to build bridges, forgive, and destroy walls of division and discord. Frequently, when positive attitudes and a conciliatory spirit are shown, couples learn to view and enjoy their in-laws as adult friends who become encouragers, supporters, and even mentors.

Common Problems That May Arise With In-Laws

In-law difficulties occur most often in the early years of marriage—the period when the new couple and their parents are working through the realignment of family relationships, loyalties, and ways of connecting. These necessary modifications can spark friction and trigger jealousy on the part of some.

When problems occur with in-laws, very rarely is the motive bad. Most parents want nothing but the best for their children and even their children's spouses, yet damage can be done while intending to do good. What are some of the predictable pitfalls and problems that can complicate the process when a young couple is making the transition from single adulthood to life as an independent married couple?

1. Parents may be unwilling to let go of a child that they have loved so long and so dearly.

It is not so hard to understand that when a child has been dependent on you for many years, it can be very difficult to release that child into the care and keeping of another person whose love and loyalty you may question. Some parents are convinced that no other man or woman is good enough for their son or daughter. Though they would be reluctant to admit it, these parents are fearful on their child's wedding day that he or she is marrying someone who is less in status or does not have the pedigree they want for their child. This attitude tends to show through over a period of time and can cause multiple problems.

2. A person who is marrying may find it difficult to break emotional ties with his or her parents.

Just as some parents may find it difficult to let go of a child, it is also true that some young adults find it emotionally difficult to make a break with their parents. After so many years of emotional dependency in a loving and secure family, it can be a frightening experience to know that you are assuming full independence as a married adult.

Gripped by feelings of insecurity, a young adult may have difficulty bonding emotionally with his or her marriage partner. Thus, in times of conflict, anger, loneliness, or financial tightness, the insecure mate may lean so heavily on parents for comfort and counsel that the marriage partner feels neglected or rejected.

3. There can be unrealistic and unhealthy expectations that create tensions and conflicts.

One mother-in-law had it all worked out. "Her children"—meaning her son and his wife—would be at her house for a meal each weekend, her son would frequently drop by after work to visit with her, the two families would never live more than 10 miles apart, Christmas Eve would be spent at her house every year, and the couple would provide four adorable grandchildren for her to enjoy. Beware of unreasonable and unhealthy expectations!

4. The choice of where to live can be a problem.

For married couples to live with either set of parents is almost always a bad idea. The old saying, "No house is big enough for two families," is a good one. Living together can set the stage for unsolicited advice to be given, unwanted control to be exercised, and dangerous family conflicts to occur.

5. There can be problems with the way time is allocated and traditions are honored.

Just when parents may be slowing down and enjoying more leisure time, a young couple may be moving at a breathless pace. This can be especially problematic when loyalty is measured by time. Tensions can sometimes be generated over where and how vacations and holidays are spent.

When an effort is made to rigidly cling to long-standing family traditions, peace and harmony within a family circle can be painfully disrupted. Beware of an attitude, which says, "The way we do things in our family is the right way. Any other approach is less desirable or downright wrong." Flexibility is absolutely necessary when the kids marry and families change. "The way it has always been" can no longer be "the way it will always be."

6. Money can be a problem where in-laws are concerned.

Strains and struggles can occur when young couples want to enjoy the same lifestyle they had while living at home. Some couples spend unwisely leading to excessive debt. They purchase on the "COD Plan"—"Count On Dad." In accepting money from parents, a couple runs the risk of losing their financial freedom. Parents who provide funds for married children may ask for financial data and assume the right to tell them how to spend their money. The other side of this problem involves parents who respond to every call for assistance.

Also, relationships can sour if there is poor communication surrounding the exchange of money between parents and married children. What one side considered a loan the other side viewed as a gift. Such misunderstandings can cause distrust and friction.

Serious problems may occur if there are employment links between in-laws. Such relationships can create daily expectations, which, if not met, can lead to frustrations and become very awkward. It can be difficult for some to exercise authority over a person in the workplace, while honoring that person's total independence in the home. The everydayness of such relationships can be potentially volatile.

7. Problems may arise over a clash of family cultures.

Eventually most couples discover that they were born and reared in two distinctive family subcultures with each having its own unique traditions and patterns of behavior that are viewed as normal. Of course, "normal" is the way it was done in "my family" of origin—not yours. The problem is that what seems perfectly normal to one person may appear as grossly abnormal to another.

A normal Thanksgiving for one partner is to eat turkey and dressing at grandma's house—the way we have done it for years—whereas, normal for the other partner is to grill steaks and watch football back home with mom and dad. A clash of cultures! Normal for one person is opening presents on Christmas Eve and sleeping late on Christmas morning, whereas the other individual knows that early on Christmas morning is the only proper time to view Santa's surprises. A clash of cultures! One partner knows that housework is for women, whereas the other person understands that household chores are to be shared. A clash of cultures! How do we discipline the kids? Who takes out the garbage? Who puts gasoline in the cars? Who decides about the family budget? Who manages the kitchen? How do we spend our Saturdays? How involved will we be in the local church? These and other such questions can lead to minor culture skirmishes or even all-out culture wars!

8. Problems can arise over the grandparents and grandchildren.

Some grandparents are so eager to have grandchildren that they let their desire be known in subtle and not so subtle ways. Once the grandchildren arrive, the matter of control can become an issue. Grandparents can run a wide gamut. On one side are those who see it as their privilege to spoil the kids rotten, and on the other side are those who are certain that your kids are going to the dogs and feel obligated to straighten them out since you won't. Problems can also be created if there is rivalry between grandparents or when grandchildren prefer one set of grandparents to the other.

9. There can be problems related to spiritual matters.

When one side of the family is devoutly Christian and the other side is not, serious problems can arise. What some view as essential, others view as incidental. Those who feel no strong devotion to Jesus Christ are not able to understand or support the Christian's commitment of time, energy, and money. Jesus envisioned such conflicts within the extended family.

> *For I have come to turn "a man against his father, a daughter against her mother, a daughter-in-law against her mother-in-law—a man's enemies will be the members of his own household."* (*Matthew 10:35-36*)

Preventive, Corrective, And Positive Measures That Promote Healthy And Happy Relationships With In-Laws

Everybody wins when there is peace in the family clan. What a wonderful blessing when family members on both sides of a marriage can live together in harmony. The following principles, if applied, will prevent hurt and promote healing within the extended family.

1. Preparation for good in-law relationships must begin prior to marriage.

Ideally, a person will become well acquainted with the parents and relatives of his or her future partner prior to marriage. Any marriage is tremendously blessed if sanctioned and approved by future in-laws. This requires positive attitudes on the part of everyone. If an engaged person decides that he or she will never be able to embrace a fiancé's family, it is highly doubtful that the marriage should occur. An important part of loving one's mate is learning to love a mate's family. Mutual acceptance of in-laws greatly enhances a couple's opportunity for harmony and peace in marriage.

Being able to enjoy warm and intimate feelings with and for the new in-laws may take time. Patience and kindness must be exercised. Each family has its own history, traditions, and language. To accept a mate's family before marriage and then arbitrarily reject them after marriage is unfair and cruel. This is manipulative behavior and can only be viewed as being self-serving.

2. Parents of a married child must understand the necessity to assume a new role as adult friends to their child and his or her marriage partner.

Emotionally and psychologically, it can be difficult for some parents to transition into a new and different kind of relationship with a married child. Ideally, this breaking away has been occurring over a period of time and culminates when, at marriage, the parents cheerfully accept their new and different role. Though they are still the parents of their child, they must now assume a new role and endeavor to be friends with their adult child and his or her marriage partner. This change can be especially hard for parents who, over the years, have built their lives around a child and his or her interests.

On the day before his wedding, a young man was moving his belongings out of his room at home and carrying them to the new apartment that he and his wife would soon occupy. His mother was filled with mixed emotions as she watched the process of his permanent exit from the home. As he packed his last few items and carried them to his car, this mom kissed him on the cheek, wished him well, and then presented him with a small box that was beautifully gift-wrapped. She told her son to open the gift once he was alone in his new residence. When he opened the box, he found a set of colorful apron strings that she had cut from one of her favorite aprons. The lesson was obvious and powerful! She was letting go.

Parents must recognize and honor the importance of non-interference. No matter what the motive, they must not usurp privileges or violate privacy with their adult children. The wisest policy seems to be that parents should not inject themselves unless invited by the couple, and even then, they should tread with care and caution. They must forego any tendency to demand repayment for what they did during the growing-up years. There must be no effort to manipulate, stir guilt, or make threats in dealing with adult children. No matter what the motive, they must not cross the sacred boundaries of another household. Your household must never be for sale. As much as we may wish to please other family members, our own family must never be in bondage—emotionally, financially, spiritually, or any other way—to someone else.

Though somewhat risky because of the emotional and subjective nature of the relationships involved, perhaps it should be pointed out that in rare cases, there may be the need for an appropriate person to cautiously intervene if there is unmistakable abuse or cruelty occurring in the extended family.

3. A child who is marrying is to leave his or her parents and form a strong bond with his or her marriage partner.

The Scriptures are clear. They must be honored.

The man said, "This is now bone of my bones and flesh of my flesh; she shall be called 'woman,' for she was taken out of man." For this reason a man will leave his father and mother and be united to his wife, and they will become one flesh. (Genesis 2:23-24)

Key words in the above passage are *"leave," be united to "your marriage partner"* and *"they will become one flesh."* In order to build a successful marriage, each step in this bonding process must occur.

There must be physical and emotional separation from parents—*"leave."* There must be a physical and emotional union in marriage—*be united to "your spouse."* And, there must be an exclusive kind of oneness that is formed between a husband and wife—*"they will become one flesh."*

4. Newly married couples must establish their own social, financial, emotional, and spiritual independence.

When God was establishing guidelines that would affect the lives and relationships of His covenant people, He led Moses to set forth some interesting instructions for newlyweds. According to *Deuteronomy 24:5*, a Jewish groom was dismissed from military duty for one year so that he could devote himself exclusively to his bride.

If a man has recently married, he must not be sent to war or have any other duty laid on him. For one year he is to be free to stay at home and bring happiness to the wife he has married. (Deuteronomy 24:5)

Married couples must set their own goals, make their own decisions, and solve their own problems. In each of these areas, a high level of privacy must be maintained. It is never healthy for a marriage partner to carry daily struggles and criticisms of a spouse to parents. Parents will tend to agree with their child even if their child is wrong. Nearly always, the in-law will be seen as the troublemaker resulting in resentment and anger, which can last for years.

While Christians are to never neglect or dishonor their parents, they are to give primary loyalty to their marriage partners. (*1 Corinthians 7:33-34*) A husband must love his wife as no other person. The wife must love her husband as no other person. Except for the Lord Jesus, a person's marriage partner is to be his or her number one priority. Once the new relationships are secured and appropriate boundaries are set and honored, everyone in the clan is able to interact in a more relaxed way. Each family is different and must find its own patterns of connecting and relating.

5. Avoid criticism of and conflict with the in-laws.

It is one thing for your marriage partner to criticize his or her own family members, but very risky for you, the in-law, to chime in. The wise course is to listen, but refrain from offering additional critical remarks. Bite your tongue. Close your lips. As perceptive and accurate as your comment might be, it can still cause problems. The cumulative effect of criticizing your in-laws may be that you gradually push your own spouse away. Comparing families is never a good choice.

Disagreements are bound to occur in our extended families. When they come, diplomacy is better than sharp confrontation. Without compromising your integrity, it is better to bend than to angrily drop bombs. Wounds can be slow to heal. To win a battle, but lose the war can be unnecessarily costly.

6. Beware of financial or emotional yokes within the extended family that could result in tensions and troubles.

Beware of financial entanglements that could stir resentments or result in a family feud. Use great caution in borrowing or accepting money from in-laws. If money is borrowed, make certain that the terms of payback are clearly understood by all parties. Loans should be repaid in full and on time. Be cautious when there are employment relationships that could be taken for granted and cause emotional barriers to be erected between family members.

7. Treat all family members with due respect and courtesy. As much as possible, practice fairness and equality.

In all family interactions, it is important to be considerate, courteous, and pleasant. To apply the silent treatment or practice isolation is always disruptive. Continue to have communication with the family of your mate. Treat both sets of in-laws with equality as much as is possible. Couples must work out a reasonable standard of fairness when it comes to gifts, cards, calls, e-mails, or visits.

8. Be good forgivers and live with the spirit of Jesus Christ.

Within all family relationships, we must resolve to be good forgivers and work hard to let go of wrongs that have been committed in the past. It is never too late to correct wrongs, to ask forgiveness, to forgive, and to begin anew. A family circle must be the environment where new beginnings can occur.

The generation that gave us birth can contribute a great deal to the strength of our households. Rather than frustrations and feuds, we must make every effort to benefit from the wisdom and maturity of those who are older. The goal must be to build healthy and mutually respectful relationships.

Children And Aging Parents

Children do have a God-given responsibility to their aging parents. The time may come when we will need to "parent our parents." (*Ephesians 6:2-3; 1 Timothy 5:8, 16*) How they are cared for will vary according to circumstances and abilities. Ideally, this is a responsibility that is accepted with love and shared by several family members. Hard decisions pertaining to their care must be made and tenderness should always be shown. When our parents pass from this life, there is a great blessing if children can look back with a sense of gratitude rather than feelings of regret.

Harmony Building Exercises

1. Read *Exodus 18*. Then, discuss the overall relationship that Moses enjoyed with his father-in-law, Jethro. How would you describe their relationship? (*Exodus 4:18*) Evaluate their ability to communicate. (*Exodus 18:7-12*)

Whose interest did Jethro have in mind when he offered advice to Moses? (*Exodus 18:13-23*)

2. Discuss the problems that you see in *Genesis 29:15-30* as the relationship between Jacob and his father-in-law, Laban, is described. What are the practical implications for us in this passage?

3. When we read of in-laws in the Scriptures, we find some relationships that were good. Perhaps the most beautiful in-law relationship described in the Bible was between Ruth and her mother-in-law. This was a strong pledge of love and loyalty. Read *Ruth 1:16-17*. If possible, pause now and do something that you may not have done in a long time—give thanks to God for your in-laws and ask for His favor in their lives.

4. Based on your knowledge and experience, what three practical guidelines do you think would be most effective in preserving peace and harmony within our extended families? Are these guidelines that you will honor when you are the in-law parents?

5. What was the biggest and most difficult adjustment that you had to make when you left your family of origin and formed your own family?

6. Powerful words were spoken by Jesus in *Matthew 10:34-39*. Discuss the implications of these radical principles.

7. How important is it for a married couple to resolve their differences and present a united stand as they interact with members of their extended family?

8. What are some practical ideas that you could share with others as to how you have managed to build a healthy and happy relationship with your in-laws?

9. Can you envision a situation where a couple would need to sit down and set definite boundaries that apply to members of their extended families? Discuss the wisdom and practicality of this idea.

CHAPTER 10
When Harmony Is Threatened— Dealing With Conflict And Anger

When Harmony Becomes Disharmony

Conflict in marriage is inevitable. The words, "And they lived happily ever after," make a nice line in fairy tales, but they do not fit when it comes to marriage. All couples have their disagreements. Minnie Pearl said, "Marriage is like sitting in a tub of hot water. It ain't so hot after you've been there a while." How's the marital temperature where you are?

As hard as you may try to maintain marital harmony, there are days when the duet turns into a duel and the beauty of your marriage melody sounds terribly off-key. After 50 years of marriage, one husband confessed, "On most days we were soul mates, but there were a few days when it felt like we were cell mates." Getting married is easy. Staying happily married is hard. All weddings are happy. It's the living together afterward that can be tough.

Dennis and Barbara Rainey of Little Rock, Arkansas explain it this way:

> "Start with two selfish people with different backgrounds and personalities. Now add some bad habits and interesting idiosyncrasies, throw in a bunch of expectations, and then turn up the heat a little with the daily trials of life. Guess what? You are bound to have conflict. It's unavoidable."

Is Conflict A Reality In Christian Marriages?

Yes, conflict is a reality even in Christian marriages. It is a myth that "nice people never have strong differences." Just because a man and a woman take a vow to be married does not suddenly cause their counter personalities, differing preferences, or conflicting points of view to vanish away. In fact, living in the close proximity of wedlock can magnify the differences and lead to major deadlock.

Marriage partners are like the two porcupines that desired closeness and companionship. They "needed" each other, but they also "needled" each other. In marriage, be prepared for the "ouch-moments." They do come.

Even though conflicts and controversies arise, there is a sense in which Christian marriages are to be different from others. Our relationship with the Lord Jesus is to affect the way in which we view, confront, and resolve our problems. When the influence of our "feel-good" culture is prompting some to bail out of their troubled relationships, the staying power of our commitment to Jesus enables us to hang in. Couples who are willing to learn and practice the relational skills taught by Jesus have the tools that they need to "work through" their problems rather than "walking out" of their relationships. No matter how long we are married, we are continually applying new problem-solving skills as we learn to practice the mind of Christ.

> *And we, who with unveiled faces all reflect the LORD's glory, are being transformed into his likeness with ever-increasing glory, which comes from the LORD, who is the Spirit. (2 Corinthians 3:18)*

Things That Hinder In The Resolution Of Marital Conflict

In the midst of marital struggles, there are some attitudes and actions we should avoid in the interest of problem-solving and peace-making. Some responses will only widen the gaps and deepen the wounds between partners. Why continue on a path that is not facilitating marital peace, but instead is increasing resentment, deepening discouragement, and creating more problems for you as a couple?

1. Be careful not to turn minor skirmishes into major battles.

The familiar old saying still applies. "Don't make mountains out of molehills." Harlan Miller says, "Often the difference between a successful marriage and a mediocre one consists of leaving about three or four things a day unsaid." Is the issue really worth confronting?

> *A man's wisdom gives him patience; it is to his glory to overlook an offense. (Proverbs 19:11)*

> *Above all, love each other deeply, because love covers over a multitude of sins. (1 Peter 4:8)*

Love is patient, love is kind. It does not envy, it does not boast, it is not proud. It is not rude, it is not self-seeking, it is not easily angered, it keeps no record of wrongs. (1 Corinthians 13:4-5)

2. Avoid the battlefield mindset, which calls for an attack-and-destroy mentality.

On a battlefield, the objective is to defeat the enemy by bombing communication lines, blowing up bridges, and inflicting pain. In war, the goal is to defeat the opponent and win a victory for your side.

In the midst of marital conflict, a husband or wife can so quickly assume this battlefield mindset. Suddenly, you are in a combat-mode with your partner, which makes it easy to forget that this person you are trying to hurt is the one with whom you are joined in a vital partnership. In military warfare, this is called "friendly fire"—you are inflicting harm on your own. Even in the midst of conflict, you must see your marriage partner as a respected friend with whom you will soon be reconciled rather than as an enemy who must be defeated.

Do not repay anyone evil for evil. Be careful to do what is right in the eyes of everybody. If it is possible, as far as it depends on you, live at peace with everyone. Do not take revenge, my friends, but leave room for God's wrath, for it is written: "It is mine to avenge; I will repay," says the LORD. . .Do not be overcome by evil, but overcome evil with good. (Romans 12:17-19, 21)

3. Don't attempt to discuss differences and resolve conflict when it is obvious that you are in a state of intense anger or rage.

Uncontrolled anger never creates an atmosphere that is conducive to the resolution of conflict. Nobody wins in a skunk fight. When an argument is raging and ugly words are flying, the wise course is to take a brief "time out" and allow tempers to cool down. Admittedly, this is not an easy thing for an angry couple to do, but the alternative can be disastrous. Make a pact with each other that when emotions are running high and hot, you will "take a break" and return to the discussion after one or both partners have had a reasonable time to regain self-control.

Do not let any unwholesome talk come out of your mouths, but only what is helpful for building others up according to their needs, that it may benefit those who listen. (Ephesians 4:29)

My dear brothers, take note of this: Everyone should be quick to listen, slow to speak and slow to become angry, for man's anger does not bring about the righteous life that God desires. (James 1:19-20)

4. In the heat of a marital struggle, avoid dirty fighting techniques.

Have you ever said, "I am so mad I can't think straight?" It is a fact that sinful anger tends to distort good, clear thinking and can cause us to resort to dirty tricks and maneuvers designed to hurt the partner with whom we differ. The following attitudes and actions classify you as a dirty fighter:

- Silent withdrawal and refusal to communicate when you are not able to agree is cruel and always wrong.

- Snipping—firing verbal shots and then walking out or hanging up—is strictly off limits.

- Airing out every degrading comment you can think to say about a partner with whom you are in disagreement violates the rules of a clean marital struggle.

- Digging up garbage from the past and dumping it on your mate is a flagrant foul. When this happens, the controversy can snowball and what once was a difference over a single issue can quickly become a struggle over many issues.

5. Refusal to apply the rules of healthy communication is hurtful in times of marital controversy.

If there is ever a time when we need to practice good communication techniques, it is when we are locked in controversy and struggling to find a path to reconciliation. To stubbornly violate these rules is both foolish and non-productive.

- Avoid a spirit that makes agreement with your point of view the only acceptable solution—"I'm right. You're wrong. And that's that!" The ultimate goal of communication must be to achieve mutual understanding rather than demanding a one-sided agreement. You can understand each other and still not agree. Unless binding truth is at stake, this calls for each partner to show a spirit of compromise and then move on.

- Avoid planning your verbal response while your mate is still talking. Good listening is crucial in conflict resolution.
- Guard against selective listening—hearing only the portion of the message that supports your position.
- Don't try to read your mate's mind. If you are not certain what your partner meant by a statement, ask for clarification.
- Allow your mate to speak without interruption and request the same courtesy for yourself.
- Avoid tones that are demeaning and sarcastic.
- Do not send hurtful and irritating messages with your non-verbal communication. With one look or movement, you can send the message, "This is a waste of time," or "I don't give anything you say much weight," or "You are stupid."

Things That Help In The Resolution Of Marital Conflict

Even though conflict in marriage is inevitable, it does not have to lead to ugly put-downs, bitter rivalry, or lonely isolation. Rather than wasting conflict in marriage, we should find creative ways to make it work for the benefit of each partner and the overall good of the marriage itself. While conflict is never desirable, if managed properly, it can actually foster healthy growth and needed reform. It can be the wake-up call that turns us back to God and to each other. Below are listed several attitudes and actions that can actually enhance constructive conflict resolution in marriage.

1. Prayer must be a vital part of our efforts to confront problems and find workable solutions.

Through the avenue of prayer, weak and ignorant humans on earth are allowed to tap into the power and wisdom of heaven. When we don't know which way to turn, when we are at a loss for workable solutions, and when the way to marital resolution seems blocked, Jesus says,

> "Ask and it will be given to you; seek and you will find; knock and the door will be opened to you. For everyone who asks receives; he who seeks finds; and to him who knocks, the door will be opened. (Matthew 7:7-8)

Just when we are ready to give up, Jesus reminds us of the power of persistent prayer.

Then Jesus told his disciples a parable to show them that they should always pray and not give up. He said: "In a certain town there was a judge who neither feared God nor cared about men. And there was a widow in that town who kept coming to him with the plea, 'Grant me justice against my adversary.' "For some time he refused. But finally he said to himself, 'Even though I don't fear God or care about men, yet because this widow keeps bothering me, I will see that she gets justice, so that she won't eventually wear me out with her coming!' " And the LORD said, "Listen to what the unjust judge says. And will not God bring about justice for his chosen ones, who cry out to him day and night? Will he keep putting them off? I tell you, he will see that they get justice, and quickly. However, when the Son of Man comes, will he find faith on the earth?" (Luke 18:1-8)

Of course, praying together in the midst of controversy is not a natural or easy thing to do. Only those who are spiritually mature and disciplined are able to respond in such a fashion. There is a tremendous blessing that comes to the couple that, in spite of their differences, makes the effort to unite in prayer and speak honestly with the Father about their unresolved issues. There is a special kind of insight and sensitivity that seems to come when you hear your hurting marriage partner pray in a spirit of humility and transparency.

In a context where the problems of division and disunity are being discussed—*Matthew 18:15-18*—Jesus describes the power available to those who agree to seek God's wisdom in prayer.

Again, I tell you that if two of you on earth agree about anything you ask for, it will be done for you by my Father in heaven. For where two or three come together in my name, there am I with them." (Matthew 18:19-20)

2. Stand united on the conviction that your marriage is a permanent relationship and that your commitment to each other is greater than any problem that may arise.

An unwavering loyalty to our marriage vows is like a heavy anchor in the midst of rough and stormy seas. This anchor holds us steady when the strong winds and high waves of conflict try to destroy the unity of our relationship. Think back to the day you married. Do you recall the general wording of the vow that you made? Was it similar to these promises?

> "I promise to live my life with you in sickness and in health, for richer or for poorer, for better or for worse, in all circumstances of life, and to forsake all others for as long as both of us shall live."

If taken seriously, this vow of commitment strengthens a couple's resolve to keep their union strong even when their emotional feelings for each other are weak. If the truth is told, there are days in most marriages when it's the "vow of commitment" and not the "vibes of emotion" that keep us together. "Marital commitment"—not "marital comfort"—is the stabilizing force that enables us to weather the stormy times and eventually find our way back into the pleasurable environment of our marital comfort.

3. Understand and be comfortable with the idea that it is possible to love and be angry with your mate at the same time.

Some have the mistaken idea that love and anger are always mutually exclusive. The truth is that in the family setting, there can be more co-existing love and anger per square inch than in any other human setting. Partners who deeply love each other can also feel extremely angry at each other. The sheer amount of time spent together in the home fosters love, but it also creates more opportunity for anger to occur.

The validity of this point is borne out by the example given by Charlie Shedd. He tells of an incident when he and his wife, Martha, were angry and exchanged sharp words. She left him a note. It said, "Dear Charlie, I hate you! Love, Martha."

4. Resolve that every divisive controversy must and will be resolved— and the sooner the better.

When conflict needs to be confronted and resolved, don't delay. Don't allow anger to smolder. Deal with small problems before they grow into big problems. Communicate! When necessary, rock the boat.

Long-term feuds and grudge bearing must not be tolerated in marriage. In healthy marriages, a partner can say, "I am angry," and then proceed to explain the basis of his or her anger—no covering up or holding on to hidden bitterness. One couple explained their successful marriage like this. "We never go to bed angry. We stay up and fight."

Better a dry crust with peace and quiet than a house full of feasting, with strife. (Proverbs 17:1)

"In your anger do not sin": Do not let the sun go down while you are still angry. (Ephesians 4:26)

5. Work hard on your good days to build a strong marital friendship, which will help to provide a strong incentive for resolving your differences on your bad days.

A genuine friendship between marriage partners makes a huge difference in the way they deal with their conflicts. Good friends may get angry at each other, but they don't stay angry for long periods. The relationship is too precious. The pain of alienation is too great.

Irving Becker said, "If you don't like someone, the way he holds his spoon will make you furious; if you do like him, he can turn his plate over into your lap and you won't mind." A sweet and solid friendship between marriage partners provides a strong motivation for building bridges and tearing down walls.

6. Take responsibility for your own sins and offenses.

Conflicts are much easier to resolve when each partner takes full responsibility for his or her part of the offense. While it is never healthy to play the role of martyr and always take the blame whether guilty or not, it is a sign of strength to take responsibility for the offenses you have committed. In most marital conflicts, there are two sides—one that may be primarily causative and the other that is secondarily contributive. It is helpful when the qualities of honesty and transparency can be so strong that both parties are able to see and admit the degree to which they have been guilty.

Conflict has a way of exposing the heart and spirit of an individual. Moral character and spiritual strength are revealed when a husband or wife can sincerely say, "I was wrong. I hurt you by my words and actions. I am truly sorry. Please forgive me." And, if the other partner can genuinely respond by saying, "I accept your apology and I forgive you," a spirit of Christ-like humility and love is demonstrated.

Marriage partners should continually be applying the words of Jesus in the Sermon on the Mount.

> *"Do not judge, or you too will be judged. For in the same way you judge others, you will be judged, and with the measure you use, it will be measured to you. Why do you look at the speck of sawdust in your brother's eye and pay no attention to the plank in your own eye? How can you say to your brother, 'Let me take the speck out of your eye,' when all the time there is a plank in your own eye? You hypocrite, first take the plank out of your own eye, and then you will see clearly to remove the speck from your brother's eye."* (*Matthew 7:1-5*)

7. Be quick and willing to forgive each other.

The resolution of conflict in marriage requires two good forgivers. Unresolved anger and bitterness poison the relationship. Resentment will even spoil our relationship with ourselves! We make our own lives sad and miserable instead of happy and full. Perhaps in no other relationship do we have more of an opportunity and challenge to practice Christian forgiveness.

And yes, forgiveness can be quite a challenge. Let's face it, when someone plunges a dagger into your heart, it's not like you have this overwhelming desire to extend forgiveness. When a marriage partner shatters your dreams, it is not always simple or easy to "just get over it." Even a series of small offenses can be irritating and difficult to overcome. Very often the feeling is, "Why should I forgive? What he or she did was wrong!" But don't forget the obvious—forgiveness is only for those who do us wrong!

A major key to forgiving is reflecting on the mercy that God has shown to us. This is the spirit we are to have toward each other.

> *Be kind and compassionate to one another, forgiving each other, just as in Christ God forgave you.* (*Ephesians 4:32*)

> *Bear with each other and forgive whatever grievances you may have against one another. Forgive as the Lord forgave you.* (*Colossians 3:13*)

Choosing to forgive does not mean that a person finds it easy to suddenly forget what occurred or totally block out all the negative feelings that may have arisen because of the offense. In most cases, forgiveness must begin as an act of the will and not a feeling of the emotions. What we can do is make the decision to extend a spirit of grace by no longer pressing charges against the offender. We can choose not to dwell on the hurt and resolve to move on. In a case where a severe offense has occurred, it may be necessary to keep repeating this forgiving process again and again.

The healing process that follows forgiveness takes time. It is a multifaceted and multi-layered process. View it not as "one big leap" but a series of steps that occur over a period of time. This time can be quick or slow depending on the depth of the injury. It is essential to remember that you must work from forgiveness to healing—not from healing to forgiveness.

Know Your Conflict Management Style

An individual's personality may influence the way in which he or she deals with marital conflict. Or, we may have been heavily influenced by a style of conflict management that we learned in our families of origin.

Some marriage partners prefer to withdraw in the face of conflict. They evade and avoid confrontation. Others approach marital struggles with a fight-to-win attitude. Perhaps they grew up in a family where it was common for people to take off the gloves and thrash everything out on the spot. Others tend to be people-pleasers and peacekeepers. Their style may be to show a spirit of appeasement and give in. And, still others prefer a style where each partner demonstrates a willingness to compromise—give a little and take a little.

Perhaps all of these approaches have some degree of merit and can be used effectively at different times and in different situations of daily life. The problem comes when marriage mates strongly prefer opposite methods of dealing with controversy. For example, a conflict can quickly escalate if one partner wants to withdraw while the other prefers to confront. Likewise, the relational gap can widen if one partner is determined to sleep on the issue while the other is dead-set on staying up and hashing it out. Know your conflict management style and how it compares with that of your mate.

All Forms Of Abuse And Violence Must Not Be Tolerated

Anger that is stirred in the midst of marital conflict can easily and quickly lead to verbal abuse or physical violence. Harsh words bruise the spirit just as a slap to the face can redden the skin. Both are forms of violence. There is never an acceptable excuse for explosive and abusive anger. Striking, shoving, throwing, yelling, cursing, name calling, and other such behaviors must not be tolerated.

A fool gives full vent to his anger, but a wise man keeps himself under control. (Proverbs 29:11)

Get rid of all bitterness, rage and anger, brawling and slander, along with every form of malice. Be kind and compassionate to one another, forgiving each other, just as in Christ God forgave you. (Ephesians 4:31-32)

Sometimes we overlook the fact that marital abuse can also be inflicted through passive-aggressive behavior. Through silent withdrawal, rejection, spiteful actions, and an unwillingness to be cooperative or cordial, we can cause great emotional pain to our partners.

A Concise Plan To Help You Resolve Your Anger

David and Vera Mace have developed an acronym—A-R-E-A—to help couples remember a better way of resolving their anger. If the method you have been practicing is not working, try this one.

A is for **ADMITTING** your anger to your spouse.

R is the desire to **RESTRAIN** your anger and not allow it to get out of control by blaming or belittling.

E stands for **EXPLAINING** in a very calm manner why you are angry.

A stands for **ACTION PLANNING** or doing something about the cause of the anger.

Don't Be Reluctant Or Slow To Seek Help

It is not uncommon for couples to reach an impasse when it comes to the satisfactory resolution to their conflicts. There are those situations where sincere partners simply cannot find their way through and out of the maze of marital misery. From their vantage point, every way seems blocked.

Before ugly wounds are inflicted and division or divorce causes permanent scarring, couples should remember that there are competent and caring people who are eager to help. When both partners are willing to cooperate, it becomes much easier for a neutral person to assist them in finding a path to resolution and reconciliation. Even if only one partner is willing to seek outside help, significant progress can sometimes be made.

In local churches, there are mature Christian couples that have years of experience in dealing with their own marital problems. Lean on their maturity and draw on their wisdom. Others may decide to rely on the expertise of a competent and highly trained Christian counselor. In most communities and in many churches these professionals are available to assist. Do not be reluctant or slow to seek help.

God has called us to live in peace. (1 Corinthians 7:15)

Harmony Building Exercises

1. Do you agree or disagree with the assertion that all married couples have their times of disagreement and conflict? Do you know of exceptions to this rule and how would you explain them?

2. Should Christianity make it easier for followers of Jesus to peacefully and effectively resolve their differences? Elaborate on your response.

3. Evaluate the wisdom and practicality of Harlan Miller's observation that in many cases the difference between a successful marriage and a mediocre one consists of leaving about three or four things a day unsaid.

4. Anger can be a powerful and dangerous force when marriage partners are embroiled in conflict. Identify three specific behaviors that are frequently used in times of anger to hurt and punish a marriage partner.

5. When there is a tug-of-war going on in our heads between "acting on the basis of logic" and "responding on the basis of emotion," which force most often dominates? Why? Does this need to change, and if so, what can we do to make a difference?

6. Refer back to the section in this chapter where dirty fighting techniques were listed. Can you add to this list?

7. Is it reasonable and practical to think that Christian couples could actually practice good communication techniques during the midst of a heated disagreement? If you have made progress in this area, share your wisdom and practical ideas with those who are still struggling in this way.

8. How do you relate to the idea that it is possible to love your mate and be very angry with this person at the same time? What insights does this give us regarding the nature of marital love? How does this view of love compare with the popular view in today's culture?

9. As it relates to marriage, evaluate the wisdom and practicality of the biblical principle stated in *Ephesians 4:26, "In your anger do not sin: Do not let the sun go down while you are still angry."*

10. What does the statement mean, "In many cases, forgiveness must begin as an act of the will and not a feeling of the emotions?" Do you agree or disagree? Why?

11. What practical steps can couples take to strengthen their marital friendship and thus enhance their opportunities to peacefully resolve their disagreements?

12. If you are studying in a group, work together in making a list of competent Christian marriage counselors available in your area. Once this list is compiled, make copies and distribute them to the members of your group. Resources like this can be extremely valuable.

CHAPTER 11
Child Rearing—Preserving Harmony
In The Midst Of Hassles

The Challenge Of Being A Parent

Someone said it correctly. "Anything that starts out with something called 'labor' couldn't be all that easy." One mother said, "The easy part is the labor. The tough part is showing up every day to actually do the work of parenting." How can we preserve family harmony in the midst of the hassles that inevitably come when you rear children?

Parenting Has Its Joys And Jolts

"Congratulations!" say all of the relatives, friends, and well-wishers to the proud parents. It is a time of great joy and celebration when a new baby is welcomed into the family circle. The experience of parenting usually starts off rather glamorously—flowers, balloons, ribbons, gifts, hugs, phone calls, and smiles. Everybody is happy! For most, this is one of life's unforgettable mountaintop experiences. Who would trade it?

However, in many cases, before the flowers have wilted and the balloons have gone flat, the illusion of doll playing is gone. In a matter of hours, we realize that parenthood not only brings great joy and fulfillment, but also great responsibility and many demands. Raw reality sets in quickly. It's the joys and jolts of child rearing.

Children can be fun and fascinating. They can also be aggravating and difficult. One couple had a rowdy little boy. They were at a loss as to what to do about his behavior. As his sixth birthday approached, the mom asked the dad, "What do you think we should get him for his birthday?" The troubled father said, "I think we should get him a bicycle." Mom said, "Do you think a bicycle will help his behavior?" The dad said, "No, but it will spread it out over a larger area."

Children can give you a thrill and they can make you ill. They bring joy to your heart, yet they can also break your heart. In most cases, when you have children, you suddenly feel a strong urge to forgive your own parents of everything. Life looks entirely different through the eyes of a parent.

The Question Of Whether Or Not To Have Children

This is a matter that couples must address at some point. If the decision is made to bring children into the world, then the question pertaining to the number of children must be answered. For some couples, this question can be a source of tension and conflict. Ideally, these are matters that have been thoroughly discussed, prayed over, and resolved prior to marriage. Careful family planning is certainly a positive sign of responsible parenthood. The arrival of a child calls for a couple to be prepared spiritually, financially, emotionally, physically, and socially. Parents who are not prepared in these ways tend to obligate others—relatives, friends, or governmental agencies—to supply whatever it is they are not able to provide for their offspring.

Always...always...it is unwise to bring a child into this world as a means of trying to strengthen a troubled marriage. Some couples have reasoned like this, "If we have a child, surely this will cause us to be closer to each other and improve the quality of our relationship." This is fantasy thinking and a great risk to the child. It is always best if there is a strong and healthy marriage in place before the arrival of an innocent baby whose security and well-being will be dependent on the stability of his or her parents.

Babies Require Lots Of Nurturing

What is more helpless than a human infant? Those early developmental months for newborns provide a unique time for a mother and father to form a strong bond with their child. Without this intensive care and love, the helpless baby would not survive. The bonding process actually begins before birth, when the parents become aware of the growing child and a relationship can begin. For the baby, this bonding begins the process of building trust and communication with others. It teaches a child that he or she is loved and wanted.

There is a critical, sensitive period just after birth that many of the child-care experts continue to study. Ethologists (ethology is the scientific study of animal behavior) have pointed to this critical period in the animal world for many years. In some communities, there are laws designed to protect human and canine populations against aggressive dogs by forbidding the trade of dogs before the age of seven weeks. This is based on the knowledge that early separation from the mother tends to make certain breeds dangerously aggressive. If such nurturing in infancy is critical for animals, how much more significant is it for humans?

Experts tell us that just after delivery, there are unusually high levels of endorphins present in mothers and infants. God designed the process so that there is a strong need for bonding immediately after birth, especially between mother and infant. Between these two, there is a natural magnetism as humans respond to their God-given urges and needs. Unless there are problems and complications, this process begins to happen in a very natural way. Little babies need to experience the warming effect of a mother's chest when cuddled. They need to know the satisfaction of finding warm milk when hungry. When they are irritable, there is security in the touch and smell of a mother's skin. Babies require lots of good parental nurturing.

Children Bring Changes—Diapers And Otherwise

New babies will almost always turn their parents' lives upside down. The addition of another human being in a home means that things will never be quite the same. In most cases, these are changes that the parents are more than willing to make. However, there may be other changes that new mothers and new fathers never fully anticipate. For example:

1. There may be physical demands that can result in total exhaustion.

Most new parents expect to be tired after the new baby arrives, but few are prepared for just how tired they will really be. New mothers are exhausted from the hard work of childbirth. They may also find that because of the baby's schedule, they rarely get to sleep more than a few hours at a time. For most caring fathers, their sleep patterns are also affected. This is why it is very important for both parents to get all of the rest that they can. A lack of sleep can lead to more serious problems.

2. There can be emotional highs and lows during the postpartum period.

It is estimated that about one-half of all new mothers experience some degree of postpartum depression. It most commonly occurs shortly after the birth, but it can strike at any time during the first year. It is commonly believed that dropping levels of estrogen and progesterone trigger these episodes.

In a different kind of way, even fathers can experience emotional highs and lows as they deal with the multitude of changes that come with the arrival of the little one. Nothing is quite the same.

3. There can be negative feelings about the baby and the work of parenting.

At times, new parents may feel overwhelmed with it all. Parenting is not easy. If a person is looking for something easy, enlist in the Marine Corp or join the roller derby. Parenting is not for sissies. Young parents need to understand that such feelings are common and it is okay and healthy to voice them.

New moms and dads don't always know what to do. Parenting takes practice. We learn as we go. No one performs with perfection. Parenting is a big responsibility, and many new parents find themselves wondering if they can handle it—even wondering if they made the right decision in having a baby. Patience with yourself, your partner, and the child is essential.

4. There can be feelings of isolation for a time.

Parents, especially mothers, who remain at home with their babies during the first few weeks, may feel quite isolated. This is normal. It can be difficult to take care of a baby for long periods with no assistance. New parents should try to arrange for temporary helpers, either from family or friends.

5. There can be major changes in new mothers, new fathers, and in the overall dynamic of their relationship.

New parents can expect to go through certain changes in their own relationship. There were two—now there are three. With the addition of each child, the overall dynamic in the family circle changes. For some, these essential changes are hard to accept and there can be feelings of resentment. In the face of these potential struggles, it is crucial for couples to remain close and focus on the positive and not the negative changes that are occurring. This is a temporary period of transition. Conditions usually get easier and better as individuals adjust to the new dynamics within the family circle.

6. There can be strains and stresses when it comes to the sharing of the responsibilities that go with child rearing.

With the coming of a baby, there is an increased workload. Parents do not enjoy the luxury of clocking out after eight hours or taking the weekends off. The work has to be done and some couples have conflict over who should do what.

A factor that may affect the sorting out of chores is whether or not both partners work outside the home. Every situation is different and calls for a high degree of sensitivity and fairness on the part of both partners. Another significant factor that can affect a new parent's point of view is the impact of role models from his or her home of origin. For example, if a new father grew up in a family where mom did all the diaper changing, he may think that this is the "macho model" for all time. These parenting models from our homes of origin can have a positive or negative impact. They can suddenly kick in when it is time to clean bottoms, wipe spills, make beds, watch the big game, prepare meals, or comfort an irritable baby at 3:25 AM. Honest communication and cheerful resolution regarding these potential differences need to occur prior to the arrival of a little one.

Other considerations, when it comes to sorting out chores, are health factors, the size of the family, and the age of the children. Each home is different and one size does not fit all. It is important to avoid extremes—being a detached parent or being forced to assume a disproportionate share of the workload. It takes two to bring children into this world. Therefore, two need to be fully involved in the hard work of child rearing.

Giving Children The Security They Need And Deserve

A child needs and craves security. It is a fundamental need for all humans, but for sure, it is primary for children. A few people and a few conditions within a child's life need to be absolutely dependable and consistently stable.

Continual excitement and perpetual entertainment are not essentials in the nurturing of children. Security is essential. What are some important factors that can enhance the security and stability of children?

1. A discernable harmony and compatibility between parents is essential to a child's security.

Few things are more threatening to a child than to see his or her primary caregivers lashing out as antagonists who are continually in conflict. Children can feel caught in the middle and fear that the family will fall apart at any time. It is scary to a child to sense that momma and daddy do not love each other. A security blanket, a teddy bear, or a colorful video can never take the place of a rock-solid set of parents who will "be there" no matter what.

Even very young children can pick up on sights and sounds that indicate coldness and hostility within the family circle. Children are tuned in even when you think they are not. They need to hear words and see actions that convey a clear message of affirmation and affection between their parents.

This does not mean that parents will never disagree and argue in front of their children. Realistically, all conflict cannot occur behind closed doors. On the positive side, when children witness a healthy kind of conflict resolution carried out in a spirit of mutual respect, this can actually provide a powerful learning experience and equip them to deal with conflict in their own lives.

2. Children need to have a strong sense of parental presence.

In the life of a child, no one can take the place of mom and dad. For children, the word "love" is spelled "T-I-M-E." Nurturing children is a tremendously important responsibility that requires a heavy investment of time and effort. Sporadic visits, rushed interactions, irritable exchanges, or long distance conversations can never take the place of a mom and dad who are on the scene and personally involved in the lives of their children on a daily basis. Nurturing a child calls for warm words to be spoken, warm meals to be shared, warm touches to be felt, and warm affirmations to be heard. Children need to experience love with skin on it. Presence! Presence! Presence!

Hear, O Israel: The LORD our God, the LORD is one. Love the LORD your God with all your heart and with all your soul and with all your strength. These commandments that I give you today are to be upon your hearts. Impress them on your children.

Talk about them when you sit at home and when you walk along the road, when you lie down and when you get up. Tie them as symbols on your hands and bind them on your foreheads. Write them on the doorframes of your houses and on your gates. (Deuteronomy 6:4-9)

When there are unavoidable conditions that require extended periods of separation between children and parents, creative alternatives must be found to compensate for the nurturing opportunities that are missed. Ideally, every child deserves the loving presence of a mother and father. Understandably, there are situations where this is not possible and other loving and caring individuals can help to fill the void. This is one of the wonderful ways that God's family, the church, can function so effectively.

3. A strong sense of love, acceptance, and family togetherness is critical to the security of a child.

Secure children have a strong sense that they belong. If this need is not met in the home, a child may seek to belong in places and with people that are hurtful and harmful. A sense of belonging is created as members of the family work hard to maintain a mutual partnership. It's one for all and all for one. They do things together. They share burdens. Each person is treated as a valuable member of the family circle and his or her point of view is fairly heard and duly considered. Each person is appropriately included in the work and responsibility of the family. A strong sense of family unity and togetherness is a powerful force for building stability in the life of a child.

Proper physical touching is an important factor in showing a spirit of acceptance. Touching is a language within itself. So much is communicated by touch. Some people have difficulty getting close to others as adults because they were never physically close to members of their families as they matured. Sexual abuse or any other kind of deviant behavior must never—it must never—occur in the life of a child.

The spirit of a child can be crushed if parents steadily send verbal or non-verbal messages which say, "You are not wanted, you are not loved, you can do nothing right, and you are a failure." These negative messages of criticism and rejection are recorded on mental tapes and replayed over and over again. Erasing these negative mental tapes can be very difficult. Replacing the old messages with new and positive messages can require years of hard work and therapy.

Fathers, do not embitter your children, or they will become discouraged. (Colossians 3:21)

Unwavering parental love is a brace and handle that keeps a child on his or her feet when the ground underneath is shaky. God is our model for healthy parental love. When we sin, He continues to love us though He disapproves of the impurities and inconsistencies in our lives. When a child is secure in the love of his or her parents, the challenges of childhood and adolescence—and even adulthood—are much easier to handle successfully. Home must be the place where children are wanted, needed, loved, and appreciated—and lovingly corrected when necessary.

4. A strong sense of the familiar and predictable is important in building security in the life of a child.

Blessed is the child who lives in an environment where there are warm and deep love relationships between parents, siblings, extended family members, and friends. To live every day in a world that, for the most part, is friendly, predictable, and affirming is a powerful stabilizing force for any child. Add happy times when family traditions can be upheld and special celebrations can be experienced and you have what can be the building blocks for strong and resilient human beings. These recurring family events give children a needed sense of heritage, history, roots, and identity.

The high-tech world in which we live keeps many of today's families continually on the move. For children, this can mean shallow roots, short-term relationships, and very little that is unchanging. Excessive mobility and multiple transplants force frequent adjustments to new cultures, new friends, new schools, new churches, and new experiences. For some, these challenges build character and add versatility, but for others, they take their toll and create emotional instability and insecurity that can carry over even into adulthood.

5. Clear and realistic boundaries enhance a child's sense of safety and security.

A healthy home environment helps children to identify and honor clear boundaries of acceptable behavior. Scientific research and day-to-day experiences verify the reality that even though children may complain about rules and boundaries, inwardly they are reassured because the limits give them a sense of security and a feeling that they are loved.

And you have forgotten that word of encouragement that addresses you as sons: "My son, do not make light of the Lord's discipline, and do not lose heart when he rebukes you, because the Lord disciplines those he loves, and he punishes everyone he accepts as a son."

Endure hardship as discipline; God is treating you as sons. For what son is not disciplined by his father? If you are not disciplined (and everyone undergoes discipline), then you are illegitimate children and not true sons. Moreover, we have all had human fathers who disciplined us and we respected them for it. How much more should we submit to the Father of our spirits and live! Our fathers disciplined us for a little while as they thought best; but God disciplines us for our good, that we may share in his holiness. No discipline seems pleasant at the time, but painful. Later on, however, it produces a harvest of righteousness and peace for those who have been trained by it. (Hebrews 12:5-11)

As much as possible, it is important for parents to be united as they teach the Scriptures, instill Christian values, and administer loving discipline. Contradictory messages and examples are confusing and tend to prompt children to exploit parental division when they spot it.

There must never be physical violence or psychological abuse in the life of a child no matter how unruly. Even very caring and conscientious parents can find this to be quite a challenge on days when patience is running low and misbehavior is running high. Recognize the symptoms early on—frequent episodes of impatience, yelling, hitting, squeezing, shoving, bruising, verbal abuse, and the like—and reach out for help before permanent damage is done.

6. Spiritual guidance and training is a must for children.

Parents are to be the primary spiritual mentors in the lives of their children. The Scriptures are clear.

Listen, my son, to your father's instruction and do not forsake your mother's teaching. They will be a garland to grace your head and a chain to adorn your neck. (Proverbs 1:8-9)

Fathers, do not exasperate your children; instead, bring them up in the training and instruction of the LORD. (Ephesians 6:4)

Parents are to teach by word and example. It is true that more is caught than taught. A strong parental model can serve as a spiritual "north star" for a child. Even if the child wanders off course for a time, this "north star" may be the marker that will inspire him or her to find the way back to God. The children are watching and listening. To seek the will of God and make a genuine effort to do what is right, especially when times are tough, tend to leave a lasting impression on a child. Example! Example! Example!

Children must know the Greatest Commandments. (*Mark 12:28-32*) They must learn, through teaching and practice, the New Commandment (*John 13:34-35*). As God's Word is lived and taught over the long haul, our offspring are to be gradually learning to live sacrificially for others, to forgive, to obey, to trust, to worship, to pray, to be grateful, to forsake sin, to be filled with the Holy Spirit, and to live with a deep respect for the inspired Scriptures. The ultimate goal of Christian parents must be to help their children *"become mature, attaining to the whole measure of the fullness of Christ." (Ephesians 4:13)*

Jesus And Children

Based on what He said and did, there can be no doubt that Jesus loved and valued children. Some of the most touching and endearing scenes of the Master are those where He interacts with the little ones. Can you visualize the following scene?

People were bringing little children to Jesus to have him touch them, but the disciples rebuked them. When Jesus saw this, he was indignant. He said to them, "Let the little children come to me, and do not hinder them, for the kingdom of God belongs to such as these. I tell you the truth, anyone who will not receive the kingdom of God like a little child will never enter it." And he took the children in his arms, put his hands on them and blessed them. (Mark 10:13-16)

At the end of a long and trying day, one distraught mom said: "Yeah, I know Jesus loved the kids, but He never had any to clean up after!" Or, did He? Don't forget that He grew up in a home in Nazareth that was full of kids. (*Matthew 13:55-56; Mark 6:3*)

Maybe as the elder son He did know what it was to clean up after messy little ones. It is likely that He was very familiar with the world of children. This wouldn't necessarily mean that a person would love kids, but in his case, this writer believes He did.

There Are No Perfect Parents—Or Children

There are no perfect parents. There are no perfect children. Where there is success in child rearing, be grateful to God and humble before men. Where there have been painful struggles and apparent failures do not lose heart or give up hope. Keep praying. Keep forgiving. Keep modeling. Keep the faith. God understands, and He knows everything.

God does love parents in a special way. He is one.

God has many children—some wayward and some faithful. He loves them all. So must we.

Harmony Building Exercises

1. Do you agree or disagree with the assertion that parenting is hard work? Elaborate on your answer.

2. In this chapter, it was asserted that everything looks different through the eyes of a parent. Do you agree? If so, why is this the case? Since having a child of your own, have you changed any of your feelings or viewpoints pertaining to your own parents?

3. Have an older and experienced set of parents share their thoughts and feelings regarding the importance of nurturing children in the home environment. Ask them to define and describe the work of nurturing. Why is nurturing so essential? What practical ideas can they share with younger parents to improve nurturing skills?

4. What practical suggestions can you offer couples that are about to become new parents that might make their adjustments to the world of parenting easier? What, for you, was the hardest part of adjusting to a new baby? What was the easiest and most enjoyable aspect?

5. From your point of view, how critical and essential is it for children to live in an environment that provides a high level of personal security?

6. Do you think you have more or less time to spend with your child than your parents or grandparents did? Why?

7. Have a least two members of your study group do careful research into the meaning of the words in *Proverbs 22:6*. After conclusions are reached, have

the two researchers share their findings with everyone. Then discuss their insights as a group.

8. Based on your willingness to share, in what area do you feel most insecure as a parent?

9. In a busy world, it can be tempting for parents to substitute gifts (things) for love and time. How and why can this cause insecurity within a child?

10. Mobility in today's world is a reality for many, but it can also be a liability for some. Discuss this reality in light of the cultural landscape and discuss practical ways to lessen its threat to our families.

11. What kinds of things do you do in your family to build unity, to create a sense of family history, to build positive memories, and to promote family togetherness?

12. How can we help each other in our efforts to build strong families? What prayer requests would you be willing to share with others? After requests are shared, make time to pray specifically about these needs.

CHAPTER 12
The Most Beautiful Harmony Of All—Spiritual Intimacy

Your Marriage—A Duet Or A Trio?

Think seriously about the spiritual climate in your marriage.

How many partners make up the union?

Two? One husband and one wife?

Or, are there three? One husband, one wife, and the one God?

Is God a vital partner in your marriage?

Is your marriage a duet? Or, is it a trio?

A marital duet is good. A beautiful harmony is created when a husband and wife function side-by-side as loyal and loving partners. Thankfully, there are many marriages that fall into this category. Our communities are stronger because they exist.

But, a marital trio is infinitely better. How wonderful it is in marriage when the two become one, not only in the flesh, but also in the Spirit. The sweetest, finest, and highest harmony of all is created when a loyal husband and wife share spiritual intimacy with a loving God who functions as the dominant third partner in their relationship. This three-way bond elevates marital partnership to its highest level.

"Unless the LORD builds the house, its builders labor in vain."
(Psalm 127:1)

Nothing...nothing...can affect marital harmony and health like a personal relationship with God that is joyfully shared with a spiritually minded marriage partner. Every aspect of marriage is improved when God is central. The joys are deeper, the burdens are more manageable, the cultures are easier to blend, and the communication is more enjoyable when married couples share a mutual commitment to God, hold a deep respect for the Word of God, and practice a healthy participation in the church of God.

The Challenge To Grow Together Spiritually—Does It Unite Or Divide?

The suggestion that couples should grow together spiritually can meet with very different reactions on the part of husbands and wives. Not every spouse gets excited when someone begins to promote the idea that marriage mates need to share a devotion to God that prompts them to spend time together praying and fasting, reading and studying the Bible, and participating enthusiastically in the activities and affairs of a local church.

The idea of actually practicing such spiritual disciplines in the home is intimidating and downright frightening to some spouses. The situation can be extremely troublesome in a marriage where one spouse longs for this level of spiritual involvement, while the other partner is less than enthusiastic or even unwilling to be an active participant. The challenge that motivates and propels one partner can threaten and repel the other.

How can these very different reactions be explained? On the surface, you would think that a heightened emphasis on spiritual development would bring joy and unity to a marriage. But, the reality is that even the suggestion of such an emphasis can result in withdrawal, anger, and division when the partners have very different views on what constitutes spiritual strength and how to bring it about. One partner responds by saying, "Yeah!" The other says, "O yeah?"

Why would two people who have united their lives in marriage react so differently? One or more of the following factors may explain the gap that can be created when the topic of spiritual intimacy in marriage is being considered:

1. Satan, our adversary, works to hinder us in our efforts to deepen intimacy with God as a married couple.

We are in a war—a war with Satan and the evil forces of darkness. His desire and delight is to block you in your efforts to build a strong spiritual marriage.

Finally, be strong in the LORD and in his mighty power. Put on the full armor of God so that you can take your stand against the devil's schemes. For our struggle is not against flesh and blood, but against the rulers, against the authorities, against the powers of this dark world and against the spiritual forces of evil in the heavenly realms. (Ephesians 6:10-12)

Be self-controlled and alert. Your enemy the devil prowls around like a roaring lion looking for someone to devour. (*1 Peter 5:8*)

Satan knows what can happen when a couple begins to unite their hearts in prayer and submit to the authority of the Scriptures. These attitudes and actions have the potential for life-changing effects. The adversary is fully aware that the very practices that would bring greater strength and unity to your marriage would also weaken his influence and power in your lives individually and as a couple. Thus, it stands to reason that Satan would oppose your efforts to move into a deeper intimacy with God and tighter spiritual bond with each other.

HARMONY HEART WORK

In an effort to understand the sharp contrast between the work of Satan and the influence of Jesus in our lives, read and meditate on the words of *John 10:10*. We must decide who we allow to have influence in our individual lives and marriages. To whom will you submit?

1. In *John 10:10,* how does Jesus describe the work that Satan desires to do in your individual life and marriage?

_____

_____

2. How does Jesus describe the work that He desires to do in your individual life and marriage?

_____

_____

2. The love of sin and spiritual indifference can keep one or both marriage partners from pursuing a deeper intimacy with God.

An intimate walk with God will keep you from living in sinful disobedience. But, a life lived in sinful disobedience will keep you from an intimate walk with God. Personal guilt is a powerful force that stifles and kills spiritual vitality.

Shared spiritual intimacy in marriage can only exist when both partners are motivated by a genuine hunger for God and a desire to live under the Lordship of Jesus Christ. It takes two. Spiritual energy and an appetite for the things of God are always adversely affected when sin is tolerated in our lives.

Those who live according to the sinful nature have their minds set on what that nature desires; but those who live in accordance with the Spirit have their minds set on what the Spirit desires. The mind of sinful man is death, but the mind controlled by the Spirit is life and peace; the sinful mind is hostile to God. It does not submit to God's law, nor can it do so. Those controlled by the sinful nature cannot please God. (Romans 8:5-8)

Spiritual indifference and dullness make it impossible to cultivate a strong spiritual bond in marriage. Spiritual intimacy is like a language. Both partners must know and speak it if they are to communicate fluently in it.

The man without the Spirit does not accept the things that come from the Spirit of God, for they are foolishness to him, and he cannot understand them, because they are spiritually discerned. (1 Corinthians 2:14)

On one occasion, Jesus told a parable about a farmer who sowed seed on various types of soil. The seed that was sown on the thorny soil helps us to understand the condition of the heart when individuals are indifferent to and unaffected by the importance of spiritual realities.

Other seed fell among thorns, which grew up with it and choked the plants. . . The seed that fell among thorns stands for those who hear, but as they go on their way they are choked by life's worries, riches and pleasures, and they do not mature. (Luke 8:7, 14)

3. Unresolved conflict and lingering anger will block the way to deeper spiritual intimacy in marriage.

The spiritual water of life cannot flow through hearts that are clogged with resentment, bitterness, and anger. Meaningful prayer cannot be shared when marriage partners are miles apart emotionally and spiritually. The Bible teaches that our attitudes on the horizontal plane seriously affect the altitude of our prayers on the vertical plane.

Husbands, in the same way be considerate as you live with your wives, and treat them with respect as the weaker partner and as heirs with you of the gracious gift of life, so that nothing will hinder your prayers. (1 Peter 3:7)

Forgive us our debts, as we also have forgiven our debtors. . . For if you forgive men when they sin against you, your heavenly Father will also forgive you. (Matthew 6:12, 14)

Wives, submit to your husbands, as is fitting in the LORD. Husbands, love your wives and do not be harsh with them. (Colossians 3:18-19)

When the physical pipes in a house are clogged, the result is a smelly mess and damaged property if repairs are not made quickly. These are always bad conditions with which to deal. But, much, much worse is the home where the emotional and spiritual pipes are blocked due to unresolved conflict, sinful anger, and an unwillingness to repair the damage through love and forgiveness. So long as the emotional and spiritual blocks are allowed to exist, Satan gains a foothold and prompts marriage partners to emit the horrible attitudinal odors that accompany sin and selfishness. (*Ephesians 4:26-27*) When rancor prevails in a marriage, the lives of others in the family are affected—even damaged. In such an environment, spiritual intimacy cannot be achieved or enjoyed.

4. Various personality types, differing levels of spiritual maturity, and diverse cultural backgrounds can account for some of the difficulties that marriage partners have in their efforts to achieve spiritual intimacy.

Wait! Before you hastily decide that your marriage partner is a spiritual dwarf and totally incapable of sharing spiritual intimacy with you, consider the possibility that other causative factors may be involved. It is important to avoid attitudes, words, and actions that create another marital battle line and stir conflict. Don't over react like the man who burned down his house while trying to kill a varmint. Recognize that it takes time and patience for changes to occur and progress to be made.

There are individuals who love God deeply, yet who, because they have a totally different personality type or religious background, are not yet ready or willing to commit to a full-scale devotional life with open prayer, verbal readings, personal commentary, and other kinds of visual and verbal participation. It is not easy for a person who tends to be introverted or grew up in a home where open prayer and Bible reading were not practiced to suddenly become comfortable with such visible and verbal spiritual expressions.

For some, there may be a high level of shyness, inferiority, or insecurity. One partner may feel that his or her level of spiritual understanding and maturity is far below that of the other mate. For others, a demonstrative expression of spirituality is simply not the way that they prefer to share their personal beliefs and feelings. Even with a marriage partner, an individual may not wish to be so open and expressive. While one partner's personality may favor such expressions, the other may not be ready for this approach to a shared devotional life. We must live at our address and relate with our unique marriage partner. To compare your mate with someone else and push for unrealistic goals is unfair and unhealthy.

When The "Spiritual Divide" Feels Like The Grand Canyon— One Partner Is Christian And The Other Is Not

When we marry across wide cultural, religious, and social gaps, marital harmony is much harder to achieve. One "spiritually split" couple admitted to this writer, "We get up mad on Sunday morning! We both feel hurt and angry, but we know better than to try to talk about it. There's just a stony silence." She would take the children and make her way to Bible classes and the church assembly. He would head for the golf course to make an 8:00 AM tee time. The priorities were very different. The gap was very wide. How sad and tragic!

Can you see the deeper implications of this situation? What you have is the believer with two natures trying to relate to and live with the non-believer who has only one nature. To Christians living in Galatia, Paul explained the struggle that goes on when they experienced the cross-pull between their two natures.

So I say, live by the Spirit, and you will not gratify the desires of the sinful nature. For the sinful nature desires what is contrary to the Spirit, and the Spirit what is contrary to the sinful nature. They are in conflict with each other, so that you do not do what you want. (Galatians 5:16-17)

However, when it comes to the nature of the non-believer, notice what Paul writes to the church in Rome.

...the sinful mind is hostile to God. It does not submit to God's law, nor can it do so. Those controlled by the sinful nature cannot please God. (Romans 8:7-8)

This is why Paul says to the Corinthian church:

What does a believer have in common with an unbeliever? (2 Corinthians 6:15)

Such "a spiritual divide" has the potential to cause so much hurt, heartache, and hostility. These differences can easily complicate and magnify other differences. Of course, the ideal is for this problem to be prevented rather than corrected. Yet, for some, the truth of that statement is only realized and taken seriously after the stage of preparation and prevention is past. The pain of this reality must motivate us to appeal to believers who are not yet married to consider the importance of being married to a person with whom they can share intimacy with Christ and fellowship in His church.

Do not be yoked together with unbelievers. For what do righteousness and wickedness have in common? Or what fellowship can light have with darkness? What harmony is there between Christ and Belial? What does a believer have in common with an unbeliever? What agreement is there between the temple of God and idols? For we are the temple of the living God. As God has said: "I will live with them and walk among them, and I will be their God, and they will be my people." (2 Corinthians 6:14-16)

A woman is bound to her husband as long as he lives. But if her husband dies, she is free to marry anyone she wishes, but he must belong to the LORD. (1 Corinthians 7:39)

When one partner is a follower of Jesus and the other is not, what can and should be done? Each situation is different and must be dealt with in light of its uniqueness. Yet, some principles seem to apply in all cases.

- The believer must continually seek God's wisdom and guidance in knowing how to connect with an unbelieving partner. (*James 1:5-7; 1 Peter 3:13-17*)
- Always, there must be major efforts to demonstrate patience, kindness, and humility. Never should anyone attempt to force a particular view or lifestyle on another person. We like quick solutions, yet this can be a very tender and fragile area.

Prepare for the long haul if necessary. The ideal is for mutual love to prevail. When love is coupled with fervent prayer, open minds, and good attitudes, it is possible for couples to find unity in the Lord. (*Colossians 4:2-6*)

- In many cases, it is helpful if a friend who is known and trusted by both, can assist them in reaching a point where faith in Jesus Christ can be mutually shared and celebrated. (*Philippians 4:2-3*)

- One of the most important factors to remember in seeking a resolution to this problem is that behavior can often be so much more powerful and persuasive than mere talk. The Word of God addresses this situation.

Wives, in the same way be submissive to your husbands so that, if any of them do not believe the word, they may be won over without words by the behavior of their wives, when they see the purity and reverence of your lives. Your beauty should not come from outward adornment, such as braided hair and the wearing of gold jewelry and fine clothes. Instead, it should be that of your inner self, the unfading beauty of a gentle and quiet spirit, which is of great worth in God's sight. For this is the way the holy women of the past who put their hope in God used to make themselves beautiful. They were submissive to their own husbands, like Sarah, who obeyed Abraham and called him her master. You are her daughters if you do what is right and do not give way to fear. Husbands, in the same way be considerate as you live with your wives, and treat them with respect as the weaker partner and as heirs with you of the gracious gift of life, so that nothing will hinder your prayers. (*1 Peter 3:1-7*)

Some spouses will not listen to the Word nor will they tolerate frequent nagging. Peter says, *"Win them without talk by your behavior."*

The Ideal Environment For Spiritual Growth In Marriage—Both Partners Sharing Mutual Love For God

What an enormous blessing when a husband and wife are alive and well in Christ Jesus—when the idea of growing together spiritually is a shared goal! Couple growth is blocked if one partner is dull or dead to the idea of spiritual intimacy. When you marry, it's like you mount a bicycle built for two. It works best when the two "riders" pedal with rhythm and harmony. A person can ride alone, but the experience is much harder—and lonelier.

A husband and wife may be at very different places in their spiritual journeys. One mate may have been a follower of Christ longer or may be more knowledgeable than the other. Where you are along the path is not nearly as important as walking the path together and sharing a mutual excitement for the Lord. Think about it. On a track, a person who is on the first lap can run alongside a person on the twentieth lap.

As you prepare to make this journey with your marriage partner, there are some important reminders to keep in mind.

1. Be aware that growth in any area usually requires that people move slightly beyond their comfort zones.

It is inconsistent to say, "I want our spiritual lives to improve, but I don't like or want any changes." If building a closer spiritual bond with your mate has been a difficult challenge to accept and rather slow in coming about, it would be wise to adopt a plan that will enable you to take "baby steps" toward success rather than attempting a giant leap that could end in disappointment and failure. Change can be threatening if too much is required, but within reasonable limits, what was uncomfortable at first can soon begin to feel good. Be realistic and use common sense.

2. Recognize that the process of working toward spiritual oneness poses a priority issue more than a time issue.

Frequently, it is our "want to's" that determine our "have to's." We tend to make time for those things that rank high on our list of priorities. If growing together spiritually is a priority that both partners really share, positive things will occur in spite of other adverse circumstances. For example, a couple that spends four nights a week separated due to unavoidable business travel, prays together each night over the phone before bedtime. There is a way.

3. Expect distractions and interruptions as you attempt to learn new behavioral patterns.

Some things are easier to begin than they are to sustain over the long haul. Discipline and perseverance do not come easy for most of us. If you strike out on a course of action, but break your rhythm along the way, do what is necessary to recover your pace and continue on. Be flexible. Modify your plan if necessary. Don't get discouraged and quit.

4. Never allow the pursuit of spiritual oneness with your mate to become a divisive issue.

The goal is peace and unity—not conflict and division. If something is not working, get off that path immediately and try something different. As you seek to build healthy patterns in your marriage, it is crucial, especially in the beginning, to go with a plan with which both partners are equally comfortable. Allowing a wedge to be formed defeats the purpose and makes matters worse.

5. Do not operate with the false assumption that spiritual intimacy will cause your marriage to be free of problems.

Hopefully, as you grow together spiritually, there will be positive changes in each marriage partner and thus improvements in the marriage overall. However, even with increased spiritual intimacy, there will still be problems to resolve and frustrations to tolerate. Author Larry Cobb writes:

"No matter how intimate their relationship, or how firm their commitment, all married people find their mates annoying or maddening at times. So how is one to accept, not just endure, an ill mannered or irritating spouse? The Bible requires that we do more, far more, than tolerate each other. We are instructed to accept each other as God accepts us. We are to forbear one another in love, and this involves something different from putting up with our mates with a resigned sigh. Somehow we are supposed to accept each other."

Practical Steps To Facilitate Spiritual Unity In Marriage

Are you, as a couple, ready to move from talk to action? Do you need some ideas for getting started? Are you ready to identify a few "connecting points" where both of you can experience a satisfying sense of spiritual intimacy? Consider these practical thoughts and ideas, but also use lots of creativity in coming up with your own unique approach.

A SPIRITUAL GROWTH WORKSHEET FOR CHRISTIAN COUPLES

Discussions related to spiritual intimacy in marriage should never be the trigger for conflict and division. You are encouraged to cheerfully work through the following exercises checking either "Yes" or "No." Once you have completed the worksheet, sit down in a spirit of peace and unity to compare your responses. Be gentle. Be considerate. The goal is to help you agree on a "Plan of Action" that will strengthen your spiritual bond with each other and deepen your intimacy with God as a couple. Approach the exercise resolving that it will result in harmony rather than harm.

EVALUATING OUR PRESENT STATUS

1. ❏ Y ❏ N Strengthening our spiritual bond with each other as a couple is a good and noble goal.

2. ❏ Y ❏ N I am willing to discuss various options and ideas as to how we may be able to improve our spiritual bond with each other and with God.

3. ❏ Y ❏ N I recognize the importance of finding avenues of spiritual growth that will be mutually comfortable and acceptable to both of us.

4. ❏ Y ❏ N I agree that a closer spiritual walk with God and each other would be healthy and helpful to us as individuals and as a couple.

5. ❏ Y ❏ N I am confident that with a spirit of cooperation and a willingness to negotiate an acceptable course of action we can make this a process that will bring us closer to God and each other.

6. ❏ Y ❏ N I am willing to put my heart into this mutual effort and work together to improve the spiritual atmosphere in our marriage.

INSPECTING THE SPIRITUAL FOUNDATIONS ON WHICH WE HOPE TO BUILD IN THE FUTURE

7. ❏ Y ❏ N We now share a lifestyle in which God is known, loved, and respected as Father.

8. ❏ Y ❏ N Presently, both of us embrace Jesus as our Savior and are seeking to obey Him as our Lord.

9. ❏ Y ❏ N Both of us desire to rely upon the presence and power of the indwelling Holy Spirit as a daily source of strength.

10. ☐ Y ☐ N We share a high view of the Bible and view the Scriptures as the inspired and authoritative Word of God.

11. ☐ Y ☐ N We love the church and desire to be mutually involved in using our God-given talents and abilities to further its mission.

12. ☐ Y ☐ N We want our home to provide a place where God is honored, members of our family are nurtured in the Christian faith, and other people are served.

OPTIONS AND OPPORTUNITIES AVAILABLE TO US FOR BUILDING SPIRITUAL INTIMACY WITHIN OUR MARRIAGE

13. ☐ Y ☐ N I would like for us to read the Bible together on a regular basis. I would feel comfortable reading aloud.

14. ☐ Y ☐ N I want us to read the same passages from the Bible, but would feel more comfortable if we read silently to ourselves.

15. ☐ Y ☐ N I am agreeable to the idea of our praying together. Let's discuss the logistics as to how we will carry this out.

16. ☐ Y ☐ N I would like for us to learn how to "pray the Scriptures." We can use passages in the *Psalms* or other Scriptures as a guide for what we say as we pray to the Father.

17. ☐ Y ☐ N I would be in favor of keeping a mutual prayer list—the names and needs of people that we want to hold up in prayer.

18. ☐ Y ☐ N I would like for us to find a devotional guide and read from it each day at a suitable time.

19. ☐ Y ☐ N I would like for us to obtain videos or audiotapes of some good Bible teacher. We could watch or listen and then discuss the material together.

20. ☐ Y ☐ N I would find it stimulating to purchase two copies of the same book and read the chapters together. The material could serve as a basis for us to discuss ideas that we think are helpful.

21. ☐ Y ☐ N I would like for us to select a biblical lectureship or seminar that we could attend together. The goal would be to expose ourselves to biblical teaching that will strengthen us as individuals and as a couple.

22. ☐ Y ☐ N I would be willing to discuss the possibility of our spending time participating in the activities of a Christian camp or mission trip.

23. ❑ Y ❑ N   I would like for us to participate together in a ministry through the local church.

24. ❑ Y ❑ N   I would be willing for us to enjoy a discussion about a lesson or sermon that we heard during the week.

25. ❑ Y ❑ N   I would welcome an opportunity for us to share personal needs and prayer requests with each other.

26. ❑ Y ❑ N   I like the idea of our becoming more hospitable at home and having guests to enjoy a meal or to study the Bible.

27. ❑ Y ❑ N   I would like for us to agree on another married couple that would be willing to mentor us.

28. ❑ Y ❑ N   I would be open to the idea of finding another married couple that we could mentor and encourage.

29. ❑ Y ❑ N   I would like for us to discuss the possibility of our pursuing a visitation ministry as a couple.

30. ❑ Y ❑ N   Let's talk about the possibility of working together to assist others in our community who have financial needs.

31. ❑ Y ❑ N   I would like for us to study the topic of fasting. Perhaps this is something that we can learn to do together.

32. ❑ Y ❑ N   Let's explore the idea of reading short sections of the Bible when we sit at our family table.

33. ❑ Y ❑ N   Let's spend time walking together. As we walk, we could take turns praying sentence prayers or sharing our thoughts on some particular topic.

34. ❑ Y ❑ N   Let's talk about a way that we could designate special times to cultivate our relationship as a couple—a night to be together or a special weekend that we spend together.

35. ❑ Y ❑ N   I would be willing to explore the possibilities of having a family night. We could think of creative ways to teach the importance of putting God at the center of our lives.

Other ideas to explore as we endeavor to deepen spiritual intimacy in our home:

1. _____

_____

2. _____

_____

3. _____

_____

4. _____

_____

5. _____

_____

The By-Products And Benefits Of Spiritual Intimacy

Gaps that now separate couples can gradually close as married partners move in a common direction—toward Jesus as Lord! Even strong-willed partners who come from very different cultures and who hold conflicting points of view can find a new plane on which to meet and share an entirely new culture in Jesus Christ. As the divine love of God gradually becomes the model for marital love, we learn to practice sensitive and sacrificial love for each other. And children who are reared in homes where mom and dad enjoy a spiritual oneness are given a memory and model that will affect them for a lifetime. As spiritual intimacy deepens in the marriage, partners are encouraged to honor their vows and live together "until death they are parted."

When the hard times come, when the disappointments weigh heavy, when the burdens press, when the physical strength and beauty fade, when illness hits, and when the sunset of life is nearing, your spiritual oneness in the Lord will provide inner beauty, strength, stability, joy, and staying power for the present and sustaining hope for the future.

Building Homes With Harmony

Let's say in the conclusion what we said in the introduction of this study. God wants your home to resemble "a concert"—not "a contest." The major goal must be "to complete"—not "compete." This can only happen when we submit ourselves to the authority and direction of our one great conductor—the Lord Jesus Christ. Following His plan for marriage and the family, we can experience "Homes With Harmony" and create beautiful relational music that will be an honor to heaven and a blessing to earth.

May God help us to have "Homes With Harmony!"

Harmony Building Exercises

1. In *Luke 8:7,14*, Jesus helps us to understand how the Word of God and its influence in our lives is *"choked by life's worries, riches and pleasures,"* so that it cannot have its full transforming impact. Discuss the meaning of *"life's worries, riches and pleasures,"* in light of today's culture and the influences of secularism, humanism, materialism, and narcissism. How are these cultural realities affecting your life, your marriage, and the population at large? What can be done to correct the influence of these evil forces and build marriages and homes that are God-centered?

2. Discuss some of the practical benefits of sharing married life with a mate who is a fellow Christian. Cite concrete examples to illustrate the benefits of a "Christian marriage."

3. In *1 Peter 3:1-7*, the biblical writer points out that some mates *"will not listen to the Word."* Peter says, *"Win them without talk by your behavior."* Can you point to real-life examples where this very thing has occurred? Find a person who has applied this biblical principle with positive results and have that person share his or her insights with you.

4. In this chapter, the point was made that working toward spiritual oneness poses a priority issue more than a time issue. Do you agree with this assertion? How significant is "the time factor" in building spiritual intimacy in a marriage?

5. Discuss the long-term risks and dangers of allowing a marriage to be built primarily on things like money, physical beauty, sex, and children? What are the long-term benefits of building Christ-centered marriages?

www.ingramcontent.com/pod-product-compliance
Lightning Source LLC
LaVergne TN
LVHW051128080426
835510LV00018B/2288